Jesus
and the
Undoing of Adam

C. BAXTER KRUGER, PH. D.

PERICHORESIS PRESS

© Perichoresis Inc, 2003 International Edition   ISBN 0-9645465-5-8

To my parents,
who taught me to walk,
and gave me the freedom to run.

Jesus
and the
Undoing of Adam

Contents

Foreword

St. Irenaeus, the great second century Church Father, in his famous treatise *Adversus Haereses*, asked the critical question:

> How could we be joined to incorruptibility and immortality unless, first, incorruptibility and immortality had become that which we also are, so that the corruptible might be swallowed up by incorruptibility, and the mortal by immortality, that we might receive the adoption of sons?[1]

In asking this question, St. Irenaeus placed his finger on the very pulse of Christian theology. Spiritually speaking, our life and our death depend on how we understand his answer. It is certain that St. Irenaeus saw the problem of sin reaching far beyond the marbled judgment hall of heaven where a public defender (Jesus Christ) argues a case on behalf of worthless lawbreakers before a quick-tempered and sovereign Judge (God Almighty). The very fact that he has placed this critical question in the context of "adoption" challenges the legalistic mindset of the Western Church. How long will it take before we realize just how far out of synch we are with the mind and heart of the patristic church? The Fathers understood the goal of eternity to be God and man in union, with humanity fully participating in the life of God *(perichoresis)*. Herein lies the necessity to think in terms of *being* or *life*—properly understood in shared relationship—rather than in terms of the law or strict law-keeping. Herein lies the *raison d'etre* for *Jesus and the Undoing of Adam*.

Dr. Kruger's *Jesus and the Undoing of Adam* is a monumental work, which in my opinion, will stand alongside the renowned apologetic treatises of St. Irenaeus and St. Athanasius. In keeping with John Calvin's principal of *brevitas et claritas,* Dr. Kruger addresses the most plaguing questions of our time, questions that have undermined the proclamation of the Gospel. He writes as a man impelled by a sense of urgency, echoing the lament of Irenaeus, to correct much of the false doctrine which has "tarred the face of God" with the brush of theological legalism. The disastrous consequences

---

[1] *Adversus Haereses, III. 19.*

of false teaching have left noticeable scars on the face of the church and have generated an untold measure of pain within the pews. In *Jesus and the Undoing of Adam,* notice has been served: The modern day evangelical legalists and Protestant Pharisees have had their moment in history.

I have had the privilege to witness the development of this book from its earliest editions to the one now placed in your hands. Though the size of the book seems but an acorn, the substance of this treatise is a mighty oak waiting to give shade, strength, and stability to the reader who seeks nothing more precious than to gaze upon the face of Jesus Christ in the proclamation of the Gospel.

This book is exceptionally readable, but it is also a carefully engineered theological tool designed to enlighten the minds and hearts of the un-churched, of disenfranchised Christians, of seminarians, and yes, even (perhaps particularly) of the present-day doctors of theology donned in oversized and outdated academic gowns. It is long overdue that the world might awaken and behold the glory of salvation as viewed from a Trinitarian perspective.

Reader, wait no longer. *Tolle, lege* - take up and read.

Scott D. de Hart, Ph.D. OTB
Dept. Chair for Church History:
Cranmer Theological Seminary, Houston, TX.
Professor: Institute for the Study of Trinitarian Theology, Jackson, MS.
Rector: St. Stephen's (Traditional) Episcopal Church, Jackson, MS.

II Corinthians 5:14-15

Preface

Twenty-two years ago, I encountered St. Athanasius' short but monumental treatise *On the Incarnation of the Word of God*. As I read his words, my imagination, as C. S. Lewis would say, was baptized, and I knew that something very real was summoning my attention and allegiance. Athanasius remains one of my favorite theologians to this day, partly because of his passion, partly because of his simplicity, but mostly because of the way his words are filled with the unmistakable living Word.

In the West, we are trained to pay careful attention to the rational, logical side of theology. In Athanasius, one is aware of a presence, a weighty presence that has its own inherent rationality and beauty. For Athanasius, there is thus an unstated rule for true theological thinking, a rule which demands respect and indeed complete obedience. We are certainly free to ignore it. We are free to invent our own theology, free to utilize whatever logic we may think is important. But not if we wish to know the truth. There is, to borrow a great insight from Michael Polanyi, a "tacit knowledge" at work in theology, as there is in every scientific discipline. We ignore it to our peril.

I did not know it at the time, but my encounter with Athanasius, and with the transcendent rationality one meets in his writings, created serious conflict within me. I was taught Calvinism from my mother's womb and heavily influenced early on by Evangelical thinking. But the magisterial truth to which Athanasius bears such eloquent witness does not sit well with either Calvinism or modern Evangelical thought. The same is true, of course, with liberal theology, but that is another story. The problem is not so much that Calvinistic and Evangelical theologies are all wrong. The problem is, they are out of step with the most obvious, yet deepest truth—the incarnation of the eternal Son of God. There is an alien logic at work in both systems of thought, which skews the truth and eclipses the staggering reality accomplished in the person of Jesus Christ.

In the profound work of T. F. Torrance, who is in my opinion the Athanasius of the modern West, I discovered that I was far from being alone. I had the privilege of doing my doctoral dissertation on Professor Torrance's theology, under the masterful tutelage of his brother James at Kings College in Aberdeen, Scotland. One finds the same tacit knowledge at work in Torrance that is present in Athanasius and the same spirit of relentless passion to follow its logic. This book is an attempt to do likewise, with particular reference to the death of our blessed Lord Jesus Christ. In some ways, the book represents the much translated and clarified version of the heart of my dissertation. But it is more than a rehash of old stuff. The baptism of life has a way of translating theology—if we choose to listen. I hope that the years between then and now have helped me earth the message. I will be disappointed if it is not so.

These are desperate times for the Church in the West. Since the Enlightenment, the Church has lost its standing in the larger culture—and its confidence to speak. I see both problems as being the result of our earlier loss of Christ-centered, and thus Trinitarian, vision.

For Athanasius, the most stunning news in the universe is the news of the incarnation of the eternal Son of God. Contemplation of such a staggering event, in the teeth of heretical perversions, led him to clarify the Christian doctrine of the Trinity. Such a move involved a massive revolution in thought—both Jewish and Greek alike—and helped forge the basic cast of mind to be used for authentic Christian thinking.

Today, Athanasius is calling us across the ages to put on the patristic mind and think, indeed to *rethink*, everything in the universe, including, and especially, the coming and work of Christ. He bids us to take the fact that God is Father, Son and Spirit seriously, and to bring the whole world of human knowledge under the cross hairs of Trinitarian logic. The Torrance brothers, along with Karl Barth and many others, have taken up the challenge. I offer this book as a hopeful contribution to the recovery of the Trinitarian and Evangelical theology of the ancient Church. I am convinced that such a recovery will not only bring renewal for the Church in the West, but will also cast a vision that will capture the imagination of the larger culture.

In saying this, I am articulating the passion of the ministry of *Perichoresis*, which was founded seven years ago in Jackson, Mississippi, for the sole reason of promoting the recovery of the gospel. It is not an easy calling, and not one that I have been eager to acknowledge. It would be far easier to sweep our Western baggage under the carpet and go on playing Church as if nothing is wrong. But such blatant denial is not the way forward, and it is certainly not the command upon us. I am exceedingly grateful for Father Scott de Hart and Dr. Robert Lucas, both of whom have been baptized in the patristic mind and take the heat of speaking against the Augustinian captivity of the Western Church. I am also grateful for the elders of St. Stephen's Episcopal Church. They are great men, seasoned veterans of life who know and love the gospel. They have welcomed me, encouraged me, and share the vision of real renewal.

In the last seven years, our ministry has expanded in unforeseen ways, not least in the birth and flourishing of our sister ministry in Adelaide, Australia. I have had the privilege of delivering the annual Perichoresis lectures there for several years. If you find this book helpful, thank God for Australia, for it was the sheer hunger of the brothers and sisters in Adelaide that called it forth. And thank God for the fellowship of Perichoresis in Jackson, for it has provided the financial backing necessary to sustain our ministry as it reaches out to the world.

On another front, the establishment of The Institute for the Study of Trinitarian Theology in January 2002 has opened new doors for a much wider ministry. ISTT is dedicated to hammering out a fresh and livable theology for our day that is both faithful to the Trinity, the incarnation, and the tradition of the ancient Church, and accessible to the average person. Lecturing at the Institute afforded me the opportunity to make the final revisions of this book. Great thanks is to be given to St. Stephens for allowing us to use its beloved Upper Room for the Institute lectures.

Finally, how do you bless those who love you endlessly and have constantly sacrificed for your welfare? To my parents I can only say: Thank you. I hope this book returns at least some of the blessing you have showered upon me.

C. Baxter Kruger, Ph.D., OTB

Introduction:
Through a Glass Clearly

Perception is not everything, but it certainly dominates our experience of every person we meet, and every event or situation or place we encounter. We cannot help it. We interact with our world based upon our perception of it. It seems obvious therefore that one of the keys to intimacy in our marriages is the ability to revise our perception of one another. The same is true in science. If we are to penetrate the mysteries of our world, then our perception of it must be in constant revision. The New Testament refers to such revision of our perception as repentance–the radical reorientation of our minds. The disciples of Jesus learned by bitter experience that human beings have a way of imposing their own ideas upon God. And they learned that in doing so, we not only create a god of our own imaginations, we also miss the real God and thus the joy of His presence and activity and blessing.

It is not surprising therefore that the New Testament is filled with the constant command to repentance. For all of us bring considerable "mental baggage" into our relationship with God, with one another and with the whole creation. As two people inevitably bring habits of thinking, living and relating into their marriage, we all bring habits of mind into our discussion of Jesus Christ—whether we are aware of it or not. To grow in our marriages means, at the very least, that we must become aware of our habits of thinking and relating, and aware of the way those habits poison the possibility of real intimacy. It is very much the same in the scientific enterprise. If we are to unlock the secrets of the cosmos, we must face the fact that we obscure the truth of things by imposing our own ideas upon them. Similarly, the way to deeper and truer knowledge of Jesus involves an increasing awareness of our mental baggage and of the way our own baggage obscures the true Jesus.

The idea of "mental baggage," however, is not necessarily a bad thing. For our ideas and concepts, our categories, assumptions and notions, function together as a pair of glasses, as it were, through which we perceive and make sense of our world. Without mental glasses of some sort we would be blind and have no way of conceiving the realities pressing upon us or of processing the endless variety

11

of information coming to us. It would be like trying to dance with someone in pitch-black dark to the music of three or four different songs at the same time. The fact that we all have mental glasses–and inevitably use them–is not where the problem lies. The difficulty lies in the fact that we have the wrong prescription. That is to say, our ideas and concepts, our categories and assumptions are skewed. There is thus a very real difference between mental baggage itself and mental *baggage.*

The crisis of human knowledge lies right here, whether we are talking about two people seeking to know one another in marriage, or a scientist seeking to know the intricacies of the cosmos, or a person seeking to know Jesus Christ. If we are to know anything as it is, and thus to have true knowledge of it, we must deal with our *baggage,* we must refine our mental instruments so that they are increasingly appropriate to the thing or person we want to know. Otherwise, we shoot our own dreams in the foot. For failure to repent, failure to revise our mental baggage inerrantly means that we are imposing our own alien ideas upon the world and the people around us, thereby dooming ourselves to live in a world generated by our own imagination.

The price tag in marriage on such imposition is the lack of real intimacy and fellowship. For how could we ever come to "know" the other person, if we are in fact recreating that person in our own image and relating only to the image we have invented? In science, the price of imposing our own ideas onto reality is the loss of discovery, with all its immense rewards. In Christian faith, it is the loss of the knowledge of Jesus Christ. Forcing our own ideas upon Jesus is a singular disaster, for it is only in knowing the staggering truth about Jesus—who he is and what he has done for and with and to the human race—that we are set free from the bondage of our profound and debilitating anxiety into the freedom to live. The hope and joy we so desperately desire, the passion and courage, the dignity and freedom, the wholeness and fullness for which we long, are the fruit of knowing Jesus Christ. It is as we come to know *him*—the real Jesus, as he is in himself as the Father's beloved Son and the Lord and Savior of the human race—that we are quickened with a hope and a freedom and inspired with a life and joy that are not our own.

It was the pearl, after all, that took away the breath of the merchant and so moved him that he sold everything he had to buy it (Matthew 13:45-46). The merchant was not acting out of cold religious duty; he was acting out of an encounter with something so beautiful, so exquisite and incomparable that it won his heart. To remove the pearl from the story is to leave the man with *himself,* where there is nothing present to rouse his passion, no glorious pearl to quicken his pulse and inspire his soul. This is exactly what happens to us when we impose our own preconceptions upon Jesus Christ. We rob ourselves of "seeing" the pearl, of encountering the one thing in the universe that can quicken us and fill us with the *life* we do not have in ourselves.

As the granddaughter of the merchant could not possibly have lived on the inspiration of her grandfather's encounter, we cannot live on the joy of our ancestors' discovery of Jesus. We must come to know him for ourselves. Each generation must seek him and find him. Only then will *we* experience the quickening and the life and freedom that our souls crave. Herein lies the crisis point for each generation in the Church. It is only by knowing Jesus that we are set free for life, yet the road to knowing Jesus requires that we acknowledge our baggage and deal with it. We must become aware of our habits of thought and examine our inherited ideas, which have shaped our perception of God. This in itself is painful and costly, but it also runs the risk of exposing the wrongheadedness of cherished notions. In marriage, to acknowledge our baggage means running the risk of exposing family patterns that the family may prefer to keep swept under the carpet. In Christian faith, to examine our mental instruments, to bring our habits of thought, our ideas and categories into the open is to run the risk of revealing the inadequacies, or perhaps even the folly, of our inherited theology. To follow Einstein is necessarily to call Newton into question. But Newton was no small man on the periphery of Western thought.

Perhaps it is more than accidental that the first words of Jesus in John's gospel form a question: "What do you seek?" Is this not the question facing each new couple in marriage, and each new generation of scientists, and each new generation in the Church? It is a simple question, really, but a loaded one. "What do you seek?" translates into: "Is it real *relationship* that you want, *intimacy*? Is it the *truth* that you seek? Is it *life* that you are after?" And implicit in these questions is another: "Are you prepared to do what is necessary to find what you want?" Like it or not, marriage, science and theology live by repentance. We must be willing to have our minds reoriented. We must be willing to rethink everything we thought we knew. For it is only as we have our mental instruments revised that we are able to see more clearly, and only as we see more clearly that we experience the liberation and joy and life of such clearer sight.

The price of Jesus Christ, as C. S. Lewis says, is to want him.[1] The price of wanting him is willingness to have our minds converted. For we cannot know Jesus—and thus experience the sheer life and freedom that only such knowing produces—if we are projecting our own preconceptions upon him. In such a case, it is not the real Jesus that we know at all, but a figment of our own imaginations. Such a Jesus will forever fail to deliver the life we seek, as surely as a *fake* pearl would have failed to take the merchant's breath away. And such a Jesus leaves us with ourselves to manufacture the kingdom, which leaves us with a kingdom that is no more than we can create. We must be willing to bear the pain of grinding out a better prescription for our glasses. To refuse to do so, to call a halt to the process and leave our habits of mind unexamined, is to run the risk of missing Jesus Christ altogether and dooming ourselves to a life, a kingdom, a salvation of our own making.

---

[1] See his essay "Three Kinds of Men," in *Present Concerns* (San Diego: Harcourt Brace Jovonavich, 1986) p. 22.

CHAPTER 1

Why Jesus Died

Why did Jesus die? Why was his death necessary? What happened in his death, and what does it mean for human experience and life? In personal relationships, in scientific enterprise and in Christian faith, and indeed in every sphere of human life, if we are to come to clear knowledge, we must seek to know things as they are in themselves. We are sentencing ourselves to mis-interpretation unless we penetrate the dynamics that make a given thing what it is. In terms of events, such as the death of Jesus Christ, we must discover the realities that created its necessity. We must understand the context of his death. Anything less inevitably short-circuits our vision of Jesus, which in effect leaves us with a "fake" Jesus, who is uninspiring and incapable of producing passion and life and wholeness. Clarity is not a luxury: It is a matter of life or death.

In the broadest terms, there are two great facts that set up the necessity of Christ's death and that function as its proper context. The first is the heart of God—and by that I mean both the purpose of God for us and the fire in God's belly that this purpose would be fulfilled at all costs. The death of Jesus Christ is part of a seamless movement that began in eternity with the Father, Son and Spirit and reached fulfillment with the exaltation of the human race in the ascension of Jesus—an exaltation to the right hand of God the Father almighty. If we are to understand why Jesus died, what happened in his death and what it means for us today, we have to go back to eternity, to the *astonishing* decision of the Father, Son and Spirit to include us in their circle of shared life. For the reality that drives the coming of Jesus Christ and pushes him to the cross is the relentless and determined passion of the Father to have us as His beloved children. The first thing to be said about the death of Jesus Christ is that he died because God the Father almighty loves us with an implacable and undaunted and everlasting love, a love that absolutely refuses to allow us to perish.

The second great fact that establishes the necessity of Jesus' death is what the Bible calls "sin," the profound spiritual disease that infiltrated the human race in Adam. Sin threatened the destruction of creation and of God's eternal purpose for us. Jesus died because God the Father refused to give up His dreams for us, and because the only way for those dreams to be fulfilled, in the context of sin, was by recreating the human race through death and resurrection.

The Fire in God's Belly

Among the religions of human history and all their visions of God, what is it about the Christian vision of God that is distinctive? What sets it apart from other religious visions? There are at least two facts about the Christian God that are unparalleled: The first is the doctrine of the Trinity. The second is the humility of God. In no other religion do we have a god who stoops, a god who comes down to enter into human history in the most inconceivably personal way. But here in Christianity, we have a God who wants to be united with us and who is prepared to humble Himself and even to suffer to accomplish such a union. The gods of human imagination are indifferent towards the human race. Towering above us in their glory, they are distant and unapproachable—preoccupied with themselves and with things far more important than human existence. These gods exist in eternal separation from us, and whatever interest they take in human affairs serves their own ends.

The Christian God is the exact opposite. In marked contrast to the gods of human imagination, the Christian God is not self-centered, not a taker at all, but a giver, and He thoroughly despises the idea of being untouchable. From the very beginning, from before the beginning, God is not indifferent towards the human race or indecisive about its future. He has staggering plans for us. Indeed, the Christian God is preoccupied *with us* and our welfare, and determined to bless us with life and fullness and glory. The Christian vision of God is of a God who is eager to know us, eager to cross the infinite chasm between the Creator and the creature, and eager to stoop down to us and lift us up so that we can share in everything that He is and has.

Such a vision of God is unique. The human mind would never

16

create a deity of such grace and humility and other-centeredness. The Christian God is interested in relationship with us, and not just relationship, but union, and not just union, but such a union that everything He is and has—all glory and fullness, all joy and beauty and unbridled life—is to be shared with us and to become as much ours as it is His. The plan from the beginning, in the Christian vision, is that God would give *Himself* to us, and nothing less, so that we could be filled to overflowing with the divine life.

Part of what John means when he tells us that Jesus Christ is the Word of God (John 1:1,14) is that there has never been a moment in all eternity when God wanted to be without us. The *man* Jesus, the *incarnate* Son, is not an afterthought or an afterword. Jesus, the incarnate Son, the humanity of God, is the eternal foreword. The relationship between God and humanity that was hammered out in Jesus Christ is not a second plan: This relationship, this union between God and humanity in Christ, is the *eternal* plan of God, which precedes creation itself. God has always purposed to become flesh. This is His eternal Word, spoken out of His being and character as the God who loves and who is determined to bless us beyond all we can think or ask. "Not God alone, but God and man together constitute the content of the Word of God attested in Scripture."[2]

Behind this vision of God stooping to enter into relationship, into union, with human beings in order to bless us, is the fact that God is Father, Son and Spirit. The Bible tells us that the Father *loves* the Son and that the Son *loves* the Father and that they share all things in the love and unchained *fellowship* of the Spirit. Nothing that could be said about God is more fundamental than this mutual love and this fellowship. God exists as Father, Son and Spirit in a rich and glorious and overflowing fellowship of acceptance and delight and passion and love. The dream of human existence begins right here in the unstifled fellowship and togetherness of the Father, Son and Spirit.

Everything else to be said about God is a variation on this theme, a description of this relationship of Father, Son and Spirit. When we talk about the love of God, we are talking about the relationship of the Father, Son and Spirit. When we talk about the holiness of God, we are trying to describe the wholeness and purity and integrity, the

---

[2] Karl Barth, *Church Dogmatics* (Edinburgh: T. & T. Clark, 1956), Vol. I/2, p. 207.

beauty, of the fellowship of the Trinity. When we talk about the right-eousness of God, we are talking about the sheer rightness of their relationship. When we talk about the fullness of God or the blessed-ness of God, we are talking about the unbridled life, the irrepressible joy and unspeakable goodness of the Father, Son and Spirit.

To believe in the Trinity means that we believe that God is a rela-tional being, and always has been, and always will be. The doctrine of the Trinity means that relationship, that fellowship, that together-ness and sharing, that self-giving and other-centeredness are not afterthoughts with God, but the deepest truth about the being of God. The Father is not consumed with Himself; He loves the Son and the Spirit. And the Son is not riddled with narcissism; he loves his Father and the Spirit. And the Spirit is not preoccupied with himself and his own glory; the Spirit loves the Father and the Son. Giving, not tak-ing; other-centeredness, not self-centeredness; sharing, not hoarding are what fire the rockets of God and lie at the very center of God's existence as Father, Son and Spirit.

When Christianity says God, it says relationship. It says self-giv-ing love expressing itself in boundless fellowship and joyous and untold unity. It does not say self-centered. It does not say removed, distant, detached, indifferent or austere. It does not say lonely or sad or bored or in need. When Christianity says God, it says Father, Son and Spirit existing in a relationship of acceptance and delight and self-giving love, a relationship that is so true, so rich and real and good, so open that the only way we can speak of it is to say that God is three, yet utterly one. For while the Father, Son and Spirit remain eternally distinct, their love for one another is so pure and their fel-lowship is so deep that any descriptive word short of "one" betrays the sheer reality of their togetherness.

Such is the Christian vision of God. But we dare not stop here. For the instant we speak of the relationship of the Triune God, we have spoken volumes about the entire cosmos. For this Trinitarian relationship, this abounding and joyous fellowship, this unspeakable oneness of love is the very womb of the universe and of humanity within it.

The universe, our solar system, the earth, and humanity are not eternal. There was a time when they were "not." There was a time when there was nothing but the circle of the Holy Trinity. The world

18

was not here, and humanity had no being, and no possibility of being. Creation—the birth and existence of the universe, of the earth and all its inhabitants, from the greatest to the lowest, from the most obvious to the invisible—was the act of the Triune God. Paul tells us that this creative activity followed a prior decision (Ephesians 1:4-5). Creation was the fruit of purpose, the outgrowth of a determined heart. Behind creation, figuring as the driving force of all divine activity, as the one thought at the forefront of the divine mind and the preoccupation of the heart of God, was the decision to give human beings a place in the circle of the Trinity. Before the blueprints for creation were drawn up, the Father, Son and Spirit set their heart and abounding philanthropy upon us. In sheer grace, the Triune God decided not to hoard the Trinitarian life and glory, but to share it with us, to *lavish* it upon us.

Why this is so, why God is this way, why the Father, Son and Spirit set the fullness of their love and lavish grace upon us and determined such a glorious destiny for us, can only be answered by peering into the mutual love of the Father and Son and Spirit. For in one way or another, the existence of everything, not least of every human being, finds its purpose in the deep and abiding love of the Triune God. That circle of love, that circle of intimacy and togetherness and fellowship, that circle of purity and mutual delight and eternal wholeness, is the matrix, the roux, of all divine thought and activity.

The thought of sharing with others—the idea of giving, of including, of blessing—and the unrelenting determination that it would be so at all costs, flows directly out of the relationship of the Father, Son and Spirit. Such love, such giving, such excessive philanthropy, such other-centeredness and self-effacing and sacrificial care are not unnatural for God. It is the way God is as Father, Son and Spirit. It is the truest truth about God, the deepest part of the well of divine being. But why the Triune God would turn such giving and care and lavish and determined love upon us is another question. Such an astonishing act is consistent, perfectly consistent with the being of God as Trinity, but it is not necessary; there is no compelling reason that it should be directed toward us. Before such love, we can only stand amazed, astonished and thrilled. Christian faith begins with such astonishment.

This decision flowing out of the being and character of God, this decision to share all that the Father, Son and Spirit are and have together with us, and the relentless determination that it would be so, is the true and proper context for the death of Jesus Christ. Jesus Christ died because the Father, Son and Spirit absolutely refused to go back on their dreams for us. "For God *so loved* the world," Jesus says, "that He gave His only Son..." (John 3:16). Before creation, the Triune God decided that the human race would be included in the Trinitarian circle of life and fullness and glory and joy. And with that decision came a fire in God's belly that it would be so no matter what it cost. The Lamb of God was slain indeed before the foundation of the world.

What was God's reaction when Adam fell into sin? What did God do when the human race and creation were plunged into ruin and began lapsing into nothingness? Did God throw up His hands and walk away, disgusted? Did He say to Himself, "I knew they would do this, they deserve to perish, let them get what they deserve"? Did God explode with anger at Adam and Eve for the audacity of disobedience to Him? Did He threaten vengeance? Did His blood begin to boil with plans of punishment and retribution? No. The Fall of Adam and Eve was met by the eternal Word of God. The disaster of Adam's sin, the chaos and misery, the brokenness and bondage of Adam's rebellion were met with an immediate and stout and intolerable divine "No! I did not create *you* to perish. I did not create *you* to flounder in misery, to live in such appalling pain and brokenness and heartache and destitution. I created *you* for life, to share in My life and glory, to participate in the fullness and joy, the free-flowing fellowship and goodness and wholeness that I share with My Son and Spirit. And I will have it no other way. It *will* be so."

Over 40 times, John tells us in his gospel that Jesus Christ was *sent* by God the Father. John saw that the coming of Jesus Christ, his death on the cross, flowed out of the endless love of the Father for us and out of His unyielding determination that His purpose for us would be fulfilled. The death of Jesus Christ is the revelation of the fact that the Father has never abandoned us, never forsaken us, that He refuses to go back on his dream to include us in the circle of life. Jesus' death is part of the fulfillment of the eternal purpose of God, part of a seamless movement designed to lay hold of the human race and lift us up into the Trinitarian life of God. For the Father will have it no other way. He will be "satisfied" with nothing less.

The Fall of Adam and the Divine Dilemma

In order to understand the death of Jesus Christ, we must begin in eternity with the Father, Son and Spirit, and with the decision to give humanity a place in their shared life and glory. This decision establishes the ultimate basis for the incarnation, life, death, resurrection and ascension of the Son of God. He became human to create a living and everlasting relationship between his Father and the human race, to be the mediator, the one in whom the life of the Triune God intersects with and flows into human existence, and the one in whom human life is lifted up into the circle of the Trinity. Through all eternity, Jesus Christ will sit at the Father's right hand, and he will share with us all that he is and has and experiences with his Father in the fellowship of the Spirit. This has been the plan from the beginning. Without it there would have been no creation and no incarnation and no death of the incarnate Son, and no resurrection and ascension. The fire in God's belly drives the incarnation and figures as the ultimate context for the death of Christ. But within this larger picture of the eternal purpose of God and its fulfillment in Jesus, there is a second reality that figures into the meaning of the death of Christ: The only way to move from the catastrophe of Adam and Eve to the right hand of God the Father almighty is through death. For the Fall of Adam was such a disaster that to rescue the human race and fulfill the eternal purpose of God for us necessitated nothing short of our recreation through death and resurrection.

According to *The Shorter Catechism* of the Westminster tradition, which I was taught as a young man, "Sin is any want of conformity unto, or transgression of, the law of God." This definition of sin is a typically legal understanding of sin as violation of the law of God. But sin is far more profound than breaking the law, either by failure to do what we should do, or by doing what we should not do. The catechism, as well as the whole legal orientation of Western theology, confuses the root with the fruit. The problem introduced by the Fall of Adam was not simply that humanity began breaking the rules. The problem was that humanity became diseased. The disease

21

is the root problem. Breaking the law is the symptom.

In my college days at the University of Mississippi, I found a copy of Athanasius' great book, *On the Incarnation of the Word of God.* To this day, I do not know how that happened. I was not known to frequent the library, let alone go out of my way to find a theology book. But I found it and read it with great delight. Athanasius taught me two things that day that have stuck with me ever since. The first is what I have been saying with respect to the love of the Father for His creation. For Athanasius, it was unthinkable that God would turn a cold shoulder to His creation, let alone turn His back on us. What then, Athanasius asks, was God being good to do, when *His* creation, when the creation that He *loved,* and had destined to such breathtaking blessing, was on the road to ruin and lapsing into non-being?[3] For Athanasius, the passion of the Father in creation becomes the fire that sends the Son to save. The sin of Adam was met by the same God and the same divine determination to bless that birthed the creation in the first place.

The second thing I learned from Athanasius' book was that sin is an organic problem. Sin is a disease, a spiritual cancer that destroys our humanity and our existence. God's answer is not to balance a ledger in heaven. God's answer to the problem of sin involves healing the disease, transforming or converting our fallen humanity into real relationship with Him. God's forgiveness would be meaningless if it were not done into flesh and blood existence and worked into real and actual reconciliation so that relationship and fellowship were, in actual fact, restored.

A few months after I read Athanasius' book, I was asked to lead a Bible study for a group of students. I wanted to talk about Jesus, about who he was and what he did. I remember struggling to think of a way of communicating the problem of sin. I was walking around my apartment thinking, when I noticed several oranges in a bowl sitting on the counter. I am not sure how long those oranges had been there, but it must have been months, for they were rotten to the core. They were imploding, diseased from the inside. There was still enough orange color about them to tell that they were oranges, but they were more slimy green and black than anything else.

---

[3] See *St. Athanasius on the Incarnation: The Treatise De Incarnatione Verbi Dei,* translated and edited by a Religious of C. S. M. V. (London: A. R. Mowbray & Co.) § 6.

I took one of those oranges to the Bible study and held it up as an illustration of the problem of sin. What God has on His hands in the Fall of Adam is not a legal problem, but an organic one. Sin is about corruption, about disease, about a deep and pervasive alienation of our very beings. To be sure, all manner of evil and wrongdoing come forth from sin, but these are symptoms of the deeper, more profound disease. If God's purpose to lift us up into union with Himself, to give us a place in the circle of the Trinitarian life, is going to be fulfilled, the disease has to be healed, the cancer has to be eradicated from our humanity. This is the dilemma that the love of the Father, Son and Spirit faced in the Fall of Adam. There has to be a radical conversion of fallen human existence. And it all has to happen in such a way that God does not lose us in the process.

The analogy of the diseased orange is good, as far as it goes, but it is limited. It helps us see something of the nature of the problem, and its depth and pervasiveness, but it is too vague, too imprecise. What exactly does it mean to say that sin is a disease? What does it mean to speak of the alienation of our very beings? It is here that we have to shift into more personal categories. We need to open a psychological window, as it were, and peer into Adam's soul, for the disease of sin involves the baptism of Adam's soul in the spiritual forces of anxiety.

To be alive, to breathe, to exist is one thing; it is quite another to be filled with overflowing and abounding life. Adam and Eve were both alive and filled, and both their existence and their abounding life came from God. What I mean here by "abounding life" is the filling of human "existence" that happens when we are free to love and be loved, free to know and be known, free to give ourselves and to receive, and when we actually move from that freedom into action and into fellowship. In fellowship something happens to us, something is quickened into being that is more than we are in ourselves. Abounding life is the fullness that is fired in the mix of knowing and being known, of intimacy, of loving and being loved, of fellowship.

The freedom of Adam and Eve to love and be loved, to know and be known, to give and share, to laugh and play, was not a freedom they possessed in themselves. It was not something, as my friend Cary Stockett says, that was "built in at the factory." The freedom to go out of themselves and embrace one another, to give themselves, to

23

expose themselves and be known, the freedom to play, was the fruit of something else. Freedom belongs to the Father, Son and Spirit, and Adam and Eve participated in the freedom of God to love. But how did that happen? How did they share in God's freedom? How did God's freedom from self-centeredness and freedom for self-giving, and thus freedom for fellowship, get from God into Adam and Eve? The answer, to borrow a statement from Jesus (John 8:31-32), is that Adam and Eve *knew* the truth, and it was by *knowing* the truth that they experienced God's freedom. Moreover, in living out that freedom, that freedom from self-centeredness and freedom for self-giving, they experienced fellowship, and fellowship filled their "existence" with "abounding life."

Adam and Eve belonged to God. They were the prized creation and the objects of God's personal delight and love and breathtaking blessing. Knowing who they were, knowing that they belonged to God, knowing that He delighted in them, did not fill them with anxiety or dread; it bathed their insides with peace, and deep and abiding security. Knowing the Father's delight, *His pleasure,* filled them with the most powerful force on earth—assurance. Their souls were baptized with assurance, and that assurance in turn generated freedom to go out of themselves and embrace one another, to give and receive, to expose themselves and be known. The baptism of assurance gave birth to fellowship, and fellowship transformed their "existence" into "abounding life."

Now let's turn this picture on its head. Think of a five-year-old girl who believes that there is a monster in the closet. What happens to the little girl's insides when she believes the monster is real? For her to "believe in" the monster is to have a razor slice through her soul. It is to be baptized not with assurance, but with anxiety. And what is the fruit of this baptism of anxiety? It destroys her freedom—her freedom to play, to laugh, to live in fellowship, to go out of her room and engage the world. A baptism of anxiety very much like this happened to Adam and Eve.

The actual Fall came before they ate the fruit. They fell when they stopped believing the truth and believed the lie of the serpent. In that moment, the razor cut through their souls, assurance was shredded, and anxiety infiltrated the scene of human history. Eating the fruit itself was the first fruit, the first response to the great anxiety that

24

swept into their hearts when they believed the lie. The serpent convinced them that God was holding out on them, that He was not giving them everything they should have, that they were not yet everything they could be. He convinced them that they were *missing out.* What happened to Adam and Eve's assurance when they believed that lie? What happened to their security and peace when they believed that God was holding out on them, that they were not everything they could be, that they were missing out on the real glory? Their assurance and security and peace were destroyed, and their souls were baptized with the lethal roux of anxiety and insecurity and guilt. Adam and Eve suddenly *knew* good and evil. Moreover, the baptism of anxiety instantly colored the way Adam and Eve perceived the world around them and one another. That baptism produced hiding, self-protection and self-centeredness, which acted together with their colored perception to obliterate their freedom for fellowship.

Knowing the truth baptized Adam and Eve's souls with assurance; the baptism of assurance created freedom to go out of themselves and know and be known; freedom to know and be known gave birth to fellowship; and fellowship filled their existence with the great dance of life. When Adam and Eve believed the lie, when they *knew* the lie, such knowledge shot fear running through their veins like lightning—and fear short-circuited their freedom to know and be known, which short-circuited fellowship, which short-circuited the great dance and its joy. And in the vacuum, isolation and loneliness and alienation rushed in, along with guilt and sorrow and inexpressible angst. Moreover, this quagmire of brokenness and estrangement and frustration soon gave birth to anger and bitterness and depression, envy and jealousy and strife, gossip and slander and murder. Anxiety became the matrix of human existence, the poisonous roux permeating the whole dish of human life, and indeed of creation.

Needless to say, Adam and Eve became different people. They still drew breath, but they no longer experienced anything close to abounding life. The lie of the evil one was an illusion, a figment of his own imagination, a legend, a myth, but it was an illusion that Adam and Eve believed to be the truth. Believing it decimated their insides and left their existence altered beyond recognition. How do we even begin to describe the problem of sin? What words do we have to describe this state of human existence?

But even more than this, the lie, their faith in the lie, and the resulting alienation began to penetrate their very beings. As Athanasius says, Adam and Eve began to lapse back into non-being. The consequence of the lie and of their faith in the lie was not only the loss of "abounding life," but also the loss of their very existence. Adam and Eve teetered on the edge of extinction. They lost the freedom to share in the Trinitarian life, and that loss began to disconnect them from God altogether, such that they were plunging from misery into absolute annihilation.

But that is not all. The worst of it is yet to be seen. The deepest problem of sin for Adam and Eve was that now the very presence of God filled them with dread. The Bible says that Adam and Eve "hid themselves from the presence of the Lord" (Genesis 3: 8). Why? Why did they hide? Why were they afraid of the presence of the Lord? Were they afraid of punishment? I think it was the love of God that they feared. It was the joy and fullness, the freedom and goodness of God that scared them.

Note this statement from C. S. Lewis, as he describes an encounter with a heavenly man in his book *The Great Divorce:* "Here was an enthroned and shining god, whose ageless spirit weighed upon mine like a burden of solid gold."[4] What shocked Lewis, and weighed so heavily upon him, was not fear of punishment, but the sheer depth of the reality of the shining god—and the way that depth exposed his own pitiful unreality. It was an exposure similar to this that Adam and Eve feared. For the presence of the Lord meant the presence of the love and joy and fullness of God, which immediately and irrefutably exposed their own bankruptcy, their perversion, their nothingness and misery. And the pain, the burden, of such exposure was unbearable. So they hid themselves from the presence of the Lord. We have been hiding ever since.

But even here, we have not come to the core problem of the Fall of Adam. The unbearable agony of such an exposure is one thing; it is quite another when that pain colors the way we see God. Adam's pain inevitably altered his understanding and the way he saw himself,

---

[4] C. S. Lewis, *The Great Divorce* (New York: Collier Books, MacMillan Publishing Co., 1946) p. 64.

his world and others, but most importantly, it altered the way he saw God. Adam projected his own brokenness, as it were, onto God's face. He tarred God's face with the brush of his own angst, which terrorized him even further and doomed him to deeper and deeper misinterpretation of the very heart of God. God did not change. God remained the same as always, faithful, determined to bless, right and true, overflowing in love and fellowship as Father, Son and Spirit. But Adam had changed, and he now projected his pain, his anxiety, onto God, thereby creating a mythological deity, a legendary god. And standing before this mythological god, this projection, Adam could feel only the most dreadful fear. For he believed himself to be standing before a god who is a hair's breadth away from anger, judgment, and utter rejection.

The Fall of Adam constitutes a staggering communication problem for God. For now there is a great ugly ditch between who God actually is and who Adam *believes* God is. From this moment forward, the truth about God will be veiled, His face will be continually tarred with the wrong brush, and His heart will be misunderstood. His every word and act and intention will be translated through the wrongheadedness of human anxiety and projection. The very presence of God in love and grace and fellowship will be translated through the fallen mind as the presence of One whose love is arbitrary and hinges on conditions, whose blessing comes with strings attached, if it comes at all, and whose character is chiefly that of a judge.

The human race is now lost in the most terrible darkness, the darkness of its own mind. It is locked into a cycle of anxiety and projection and misperception. The fallen mind not only projects its anxiety on the world and the people around it; the greatest disaster is that it projects its brokenness onto God's face. Moreover, it then interprets God's every move through that projection. How will God ever get through and communicate the truth about who He is? What God says is one thing, what we *hear* is quite another. For what we hear is inevitably shaped by our own anxiety and by our mythology, by the legendary god of our anxious imaginations. The revelation of God to us, irrespective of how powerful and clear it may be from God's side, is always perceived through our "mental glasses," which are now thoroughly foreign to God, indeed antithetical to the divine truth. How will God ever penetrate the veil of the fallen mind? How will the human race ever know the real God and share in the fellowship of the Father, Son and Spirit? And even if God does get through to the fallen mind, there remains the problem of the unbearable agony that the presence of the Lord stirs up as its exposes our bankruptcy. This is the dilemma that the unending love of God faces in the Fall of Adam.

Israel as the Womb of the Incarnation

The response of the Father, Son and Spirit to Adam's plunge into utter ruin can be put into one word: "No!" In that "No" echoes the eternal "Yes" of the Trinity to us. Creation flows out of the circle of divine sharing and out of the decision, the determined decision, to share the Triune life with human beings. That will of God for our blessing, that determined "Yes" to us, translates into an intolerable "No!" in the teeth of the Fall. God is *for us* and therefore opposed—utterly, eternally and passionately opposed—to our destruction. That opposition, that fiery and passionate and determined "No!" to the disaster of the Fall, is the proper understanding of the wrath of God. Wrath is not the opposite of love. Wrath is the love of God in action, in opposing action. It is precisely because the Triune God has spoken an eternal "Yes!" to the human race, a "Yes!" to life and fullness and joy for us, that the Fall and its disaster is met with a stout and intolerable "No! This is not acceptable. I did not create *you* for misery." Therein the plan of reconciliation begins to unfold.

God calls Abraham, and through Abraham establishes a nation, and with that nation He begins a long and necessarily painful relationship. First, He gives the law through Moses to check the chaos of the Fall, and to help the Israelites begin to understand that there is a serious problem. The law, however, was never the point. The point was God and Israel in relationship—the living God drawing near to fallen Adamic existence in the people of Israel. The calling of Israel was not about God dispensing accurate information about Himself so that the Israelites could have a good theology; the calling of Israel was about God Himself re-entering into contact, into living fellowship and personal relationship with fallen Adam.

One of T. F. Torrance's great contributions to Christian thought is the way he understands the gut-wrench of Israel's existence.[5] Whereas Adam and Eve hid in the bushes from God, Israel was called into fellowship with God Himself. Israel had to bear the unbearable—a real relationship, not with the law, but with God. On the one side, there was the Father, Son and Spirit and their fellowship and intimacy, their unbounded life and joy and wholeness. On the other side, there was Israel, fallen, corrupt and estranged, alienated, broken and fearful—and projecting all of its fears onto God's face. How could a real relationship between God and Israel even be possible?

Again and again, Israel bolted for the door to run away. The goodness of God, the love and joy and glory of God, were too much to bear. Like Adam and Eve, the Israelites tried to hide from the presence of the Lord. They tried to create a religion to keep God at a safe distance. They tried to be like the nations around them. But God would not let them go. The remarkable thing about Israel's history is that here we have a people from the fallen world of Adam, a people estranged and scared out of their wits, thrown into the room with God Himself. Think again of Lewis' statement: "Here was an enthroned and shining god, whose ageless spirit weighed upon mine like a burden of solid gold." Israel was locked into a relationship not with abstract truths about God, but *with God Himself.* Far from merely rippling the surface of Israel's intellect, the revelation of God meant a divine invasion into Israel's existence. It meant the very real presence of the living God, which weighed upon Israel as the burden of all burdens.

The harrowing and painful ordeal of God's relationship with fallen Israel produced two great realities. First, it established a bridgehead inside the estranged mind of fallen humanity. In the creative genius of the Spirit, the revelation of God began to penetrate Israel's projections and wrongheadedness and paganism. As such, it acted as a refining fire, burning away Israel's diseased thinking and being. The living Word wrestled with Israel's fallen mind and began to

---

[5] See *The Mediation of Christ* (Grand Rapids: Eerdmans, 1983), *God and Rationality,* (London: Oxford University Press, 1971), Chapter 6: "The Word of God and the Response of Man," "Salvation Is of the Jews" [EQ vol. 22 (1950) pp. 164-173] and "Israel and the Incarnation" [Judica vol. 13 (1957) pp. 1-18].

clothe itself in human thoughts and ideas. The fruit of such wrestling and conflict was the forging of new concepts and ideas such as covenant, faithfulness, sin, atonement, mercy, community, and prophet, priest and king, all of which would become "the essential furniture of our knowledge of God,"[6] as Torrance puts it. These concepts and ideas, forged through the fire of revelation in the fallen mind of Israel, would become the new mental instruments or the pair of glasses through which the world could begin to see the truth about God and enter into living and meaningful fellowship with the Father.

Second, the real presence of God in the midst of fallen Israel created a stir that was to become the matrix of the incarnation itself. In Israel, the Word of God was already "on the road to becoming flesh,"[7] as Torrance says. For revelation means nothing less than the unveiling of God Himself—not merely truths about God—and thus revelation means a living encounter that presses for fulfillment in response and in knowing and fellowship, in embodiment. The living Word of God finds its true fulfillment not only in clothing itself in human words and thoughts, but in translating itself into flesh and blood existence. By its very nature, the revelation of God would not allow Israel to sweep her brokenness under the carpet. There could be no hiding, no denial, no religion. The real presence of God thus stirred up all manner of conflict with Israel, for it infallibly brought the Fall of Adam to the surface in Israel's existence—and created the fight of fights.

This conflict between God and Israel is nothing less than the prehistory of atonement and reconciliation, the first flashes of the impossible union between God and fallen humanity. For it was Israel—*fallen Israel*—in all of her alienation, who was summoned into the presence of the Lord and called to take real steps into fellowship with the true and living God. The contradiction and the fellowship created by the revelation of God to Israel in her darkness and alienation constitute the first form of death and resurrection; the first hint of the end and the new beginning of fallen Adamic existence, of the new covenant, of Pentecost and the coming of the Kingdom of God. But more than this, the conflict created by the unveiling of God to fallen

---

[6] Thomas F. Torrance, *The Mediation of Christ* (Grand Rapids: Eerdmans, 1983) p. 20.

[7] *Conflict and Agreement in the Church* (London: Lutterworth Press, 1959) vol. 1, p. 266.

Israel establishes the womb of the incarnation[8] itself, the living situation, the unbearable and agonizing tension into which the Son of God himself would be born.

The Conversion of Adamic Existence in Jesus Christ

To think of the ascension of Jesus Christ into heaven, to think of him seated now and forever at the right hand of God the Father almighty, as the Creed says, and to think of the ascension in the context of the Fall of Adam and in the context of Israel's conflict with God, is to stand before the miracle of the work of Jesus Christ. The ascension means that now and forever a human being, a Jew, a son of Adam, is face to face with the Father. Now and forever, one from the foreign world of Adam lives in fellowship, indeed in utter union, with God the Father, sharing all things with the Father in the unrestrained fellowship of the Spirit.

Sitting at the right hand of God the Father almighty is the exact opposite of hiding in the bushes in the Garden of Eden. It is the exact opposite of Israel running from God, of religion. The ascension preaches to us that here in Jesus Christ, the incarnate Son of God, the Fall of Adam and Eve has been undone, Adamic existence has been thoroughly converted to God, fundamentally reordered into right relationship with God. Moreover, the ascension of Christ preaches that God and Israel have been reconciled and that the evil one with his enslaving lie has been decisively defeated. Fellowship, not contradiction or conflict, now fills the covenant. Truth, not the illusion of the evil one, now dominates the relationship between God and human existence in Jesus Christ.

The Christian church has always confessed that Jesus Christ is God come in the flesh, fully divine and fully human, God of God and man of man. It is in thinking these two truths together that we come to the heart of the work of Jesus Christ. The sum and substance of

---

[8] The phrase is adapted from T. F. Torrance. See *God and Rationality,* (London: Oxford University Press, 1971) p. 149; *Reality and Evangelical Theology* (Philadelphia: Westminster Press, 1982) p. 87 and *Theology in Reconstruction,* Chapter 8: "The Place of Christology in Biblical and Dogmatic Theology" (Grand Rapids: Wm B. Eerdmands Pub. Co., 1985) p. 145.

the work of Christ is that the eternal Son of God became human and lived out his divine sonship inside our fallen Adamic existence, and in so doing not only converted fallen Adamic existence, but also forged a real and abiding relationship, a union, between God the Father and fallen humanity.

On the one side, there is the truth that Jesus Christ is the eternal Son of God, the Father's beloved, who from all eternity has loved the Father with all of his heart, soul, mind and strength, and shared all things with Him in the untold fellowship of the Spirit. The incarnation is not merely about some generic divine being becoming human. The Christian Church confesses nothing of an abstract divinity, a "lone ranger" god who dwells in isolation. The confession of the Christian Church is that God is Father, Son and Spirit. It was not a god, but the *Son* of God, who became human. The incarnation, therefore, is the act of the Triune God, and it means nothing short of the earthing of the eternal trinitarian fellowship. When the Son of God stepped across the divide and entered into human existence, he did not leave his Father or the Spirit behind. The incarnation means that the very life of the Trinity—the fellowship and camaraderie and togetherness, the fullness and joy and glory of the Father, Son and Spirit, and nothing less—set up shop inside human existence.

On the other side, there is the staggering truth that the Son of God became *flesh,* as John tells us (John 1:14). It is one thing to say that the Son of God became a human being; it is quite another to say that he became *flesh.* "Flesh" locates the incarnation not only within human existence, but within the pale of fallen Adamic existence. It could not have been otherwise. Jesus' mission was to bring the *fallen* human race to the right hand of God the Father almighty. His mission was to reconcile *us* to God, to heal the breach, to undo the Fall and bring us to glory. The mind-boggling truth of the incarnation is that the Son of God stepped right into the stream of the Fall. He entered into the quagmire of human estrangement and alienation from God. We do not understand the incarnation until we see that the Son of God entered into fallen Adam's skin and took upon himself Adam's estranged and alienated mind.

Both truths have to be held together or everything is lost. If Jesus Christ ceases to be the Father's beloved Son who lives in fellowship with the Father in the Spirit, then he has nothing to give to fallen humanity. Indeed, if that fellowship is broken, then Jesus would become just another man estranged from God. On the other hand, if the Son of God fails to penetrate Adam's alienation, fails to enter into our brokenness and estrangement and perversion, then he may have all the blessings of God, but they do not reach *us*. Adamic existence remains untouched, unhealed, unsaved. The covenant relationship between God and Israel remains one of conflict and contradiction, and the human race remains in the illusion of the evil one—lost to God.

The existence of the universe and of the human race within it is not an accident. The Triune God created the world as the first act of a vast and almost inconceivably gracious scheme to lift the human race into the circle of the Trinitarian life itself. Creation serves the higher purpose of adoption. Unto this end the incarnation of the Son was predestined, for there could never be a union between the Trinity and humanity without the most profound stooping on God's part–a stooping which would establish real and actual union between the life of God and human existence. So Paul tells us that we were pre-destined to adoption before the foundation of the world *and* that our adoption was predestined to be accomplished "through Jesus Christ" (Ephesians 1:5). Adoption is the eternal point. Creation is the begin-ning, the first step toward its fulfillment, which prepares the way for the incarnation of the Son and the accomplishment of our adoption in him. The Fall of Adam means that the incarnation will be an ago-nizing event, and one that involves untold risk. If the Son of God enters into Adam's world and takes on Adam's fallen mind, there is a very real chance that he will believe in the god who appears there and begin to live out of that appearance, thereby violating his eternal relationship with the Father in the Spirit. What is at stake in the incarnation is the very being of God and thus the existence of the uni-verse, on the one hand, and the salvation of the human race on the other. In astounding grace, the Triune God hazards its very being for us and our blessing.

The incarnation means that although he is the eternal and beloved Son, and although he is baptized with the Spirit and receives his witness, Jesus sees what Adam sees. In entering into Adam's world, the Son of God enters into Adam's fallen mind. He puts on Adam's glasses, the ones that mar God's face and fill the Father's eyes with indifference, or with disgust, judgment and rejection. Whatever it was that Adam projected onto God, and whatever it was that he felt when he did so, Jesus saw and felt, and he saw it and felt it with the same intensity and reality as Adam.

The paradox at the heart of Christianity is that the Son of God entered into fallen Adamic existence without ceasing to be the Son of God. He became Adam without ceasing to be the faithful Son of the Father. The life of the Trinity intersected the brokenness of fallen human existence. How is this possible? How could the fellowship of the Trinity penetrate Adam's hiding? How could the togetherness and integrity of the Father, Son and Spirit enter into the brokenness and perversion of fallen Adamic existence? How could the one who knows the Father and loves Him with all of his heart enter into the wrongheadedness and blindness and projections of Adam and of Israel? How could this contradiction be possible?

The answer is that it is not possible—something has to give, something has to change. Either the fellowship of the Father, Son and Spirit grinds to an eternal halt, or Adamic existence is fundamentally reordered. Either the love of the Triune God is broken, or Adamic flesh is converted to God. There has to be a conversion, a fundamental restructuring either in the being and character of God, or in the being and character of Adam.

The entrance of the fellowship of the Father, Son and Spirit into our alienation and estrangement did not mean the ruin of the Trinity—it meant war. As Luke tells us, Jesus Christ beat his way forward by blows. The Son of God entered into our broken, fallen, alienated human existence. He took upon himself our fallen flesh. He stood in Adam's shoes, in Israel's shoes, in our shoes, and he steadfastly refused to be like Adam. He refused to be like Israel. He entered into fallen human existence and steadfastly refused to be "fallen" in it. Step by step, blow by blow, moment by moment, he refused to believe in the god of Adam and he loved his Father with all of his heart, soul, mind, and strength. Step by step, blow by blow, moment by moment, he hammered out his sonship on the anvil of fallen Adamic existence. Step by step, blow by blow, moment by moment, he bent back the thoroughgoing wrongheadedness of the Adamic mind.

It took 33 years of fire and trial, of temptation, with loud crying and tears. What we see in Gethsemane, the gut-wrench of it all, the pain and overwhelming weight, the struggle, the passion, the agony, is a window into the whole life of Jesus Christ. To relegate the suffering of Jesus Christ, the agony that he bore, to a few infinite moments on the cross is to miss the point entirely. His whole life was a harrowing ordeal of struggle, of suffering, of trial and tribulation and pain. For he lived out his sonship inside nothing less than fallen Adamic existence. His whole life was a perpetual cross—and resurrection.

The death of Jesus Christ was not punishment from the hands of an angry God; it was the Son's ultimate identification with fallen Adam, and the supreme expression of faithfulness to his own identity as the One who lives in fellowship with the Father in the Spirit. For he truly entered into our brokenness and estrangement and alienation. He bore the intolerable contradiction in his own being, and he resolved it through fire and trial, by dying to his Adamic flesh, by crucifying it on Calvary. For in no other way could he live out his fellowship with his Father—as the *incarnate* Son, in the teeth of the Fall—except through the radical circumcision of his Adamic flesh and the complete undoing of the Adamic mind.

The intolerable "No!" shouted by God at the Fall translated into incarnation and into the personal refusal of Jesus Christ to live in darkness: "I will not walk in darkness, I will not believe in Adam's mythological god, I will not forsake my Father, I will not turn my back on the Spirit." And more important, the "No!" of God to the Fall translated into the "Yes!" of the incarnate Son: "I will love my Father with all of my heart, soul, mind, and strength. I will live in the Holy Spirit. I will be true to myself as the Father's beloved." The price tag on that "Yes!" was 33 years of suffering, in and through which the incarnate Son was steadily turning Adamic existence inside out, steadily bending back the estrangement of the Fall, steadily reordering human relationship with God. There on the cross, it all came to a triumphal end. There, he took the decisive step in converting Adamic flesh. There, he shouted his final and decisive "No!" to Adam and to Adam's legendary god, and his final and decisive "Yes!" to his Father. He died—and fallen Adamic existence died with him.

On the cross, Jesus penetrated to the root of Adam's estrangement. There, he walked into the unimaginable abyss of Adam's alienation, where Adam's guts were wrenching with fear, where the razor had cut through Adam's soul, where he had tarred God's face with the horrid brush and stood terrorized at such a sight, where Adam could only feel abandoned and rejected, despised and utterly forsaken by God. On the cross, Jesus experienced the terrifying hell of Adamic mythology to the uttermost, crying out in agony, "My God, My God, why have You forsaken me?" But it was precisely there, precisely in the unimaginable abyss of that unspeakable pain, that Jesus Christ refused to believe the lie, and he knew and loved his Father. The final word was not, "My God, My God, why have you forsaken me?" The final word was, "Father, into Your hands I commend my Spirit." Even there, *especially* there, in the teeth of Adam's projection, in the belly of human alienation, the fellowship of the Father, Son and Spirit won out.

What emerged on the other side of the cross is a man—the divine son incarnate, to be sure, but the son *as man*—a human being from the world lost in Adam's mythology, who knows and loves the Father; a man from the belly of alienation who rose in face-to-face fellowship with God the Father almighty; a man from Adam's seed in whom no trace of the Fall can be found; a man who lives forever in real fellowship with the Father in the baptism of the Spirit.

The death of Jesus Christ was not the end of the divine relationship of the Father, Son and Spirit; it was its absolute triumph. For dying on the cross was the Son's final and decisive refusal to be Adam and to live in Adam's world. As such, the death of Christ was the radical circumcision of Adamic flesh, the end of human estrangement from God, the final act of a fundamental reordering of the fallen mind into union and fellowship with God. In Jesus Christ, Adam and fallen Adamic existence came to an end—and to a new beginning.

Jesus Christ is not a divine tool that God picked up and used for a while and then put back in the heavenly toolbox. And he most certainly is not a mere accountant who balances a legal ledger in heaven. Jesus Christ is living reconciliation, living atonement. He is man, from the lost world of Adam's darkness, now and forever right with God the Father. He is Adamic man, now and forever at-one with the Father, living in union and communion with the Father, accepted and embraced by the Father and seated at his right hand in the fellowship of the Spirit.

Why did Jesus Christ die? He died because the Triune God loves us with an everlasting and passionate love, because the Triune God absolutely refuses to allow us to be destroyed. He died because the only way to get from the Fall of Adam to the right hand of God the Father almighty was through the recreation of Adamic existence that required the incarnation of the Triune life of God, 33 years of struggle and suffering, and the crucifixion and resurrection of Adamic flesh.

The *Good* News

But even here, we are only scratching the surface of the meaning of Jesus Christ. Does the New Testament leave us staring at the ascension of Jesus wondering how we are going to follow Jesus? Was all of this hammered out through fire and trial so that we would have a great example to follow? If we stop here with the death and resurrection and ascension of Christ, we may have Adamic existence converted to God, we may have one from the fallen world of Adam seated at the Father's right hand and living in the fellowship of the Spirit, but we still have no gospel, and the eternal purpose of the Triune God for *us* is still unfulfilled. For as yet, we are still spectators, still on the outside looking in.

The deepest joy of the New Testament lies precisely in the fact that it sees that in this *one* man, Jesus Christ, God was dealing not just with Adam or with a general Adamic existence, but with the whole human race. The New Testament does not leave us contemplating Jesus Christ from a distance. It leaves us seeing ourselves crucified with Christ, and raised up with him, and seated with him at the Father's right hand. The apostle Paul sums it up in the simplest and most stunning statement in 2 Corinthians 5:14. Paul tells us that he reached a conclusion that changed both his own life and the way he saw history and every human being within it. The conclusion was that "...one died for all, therefore all died...." It was Jesus Christ alone who died and who rose again, but Paul sees clearly that the whole human race was bound up in what happened to Jesus Christ.

Paul does not explain how this could be; he is just thrilled and awed that it is. He sees that in this one man, God gathered the whole human race together. There are hints of this gathering, this connection, in the Old Testament. Think of the High Priest's ministry in the holy of holies, where he represented all of Israel, such that what happened to him in that holy place happened to Israel. Think of the story of David and Goliath, where the futures of the two respective nations were bound up in the outcome of the battle between these two men. If Goliath won, then the Israelites would be the slaves of the Philistines. If David won, then the Philistines would be the slaves of the Israelites. Think of the figure of Adam, whose fall had such momentous implications for all of humanity. The connection between the High Priest and Israel, David and Goliath and their nations, Adam and humanity, foreshadows the connection between Jesus Christ and humanity. Adam was a mere type, as Paul says, of Jesus (Romans 5:14), the real Head and Lord of the human race.

Underneath Paul's conclusion that "one died for all, therefore all died," and underneath John's proclamation that Jesus is the Lamb of God who takes away the sin of the world, and underneath the New Testament's declaration that Jesus Christ is Lord lies the foundational truth that there is a decisive connection between Jesus Christ and the human race. We were and are bound up in him and in what became of him. We were implicated in what happened to Jesus, so much so that *our* identity, *our* existence, *our* past, present and future, *our* relationship with God and with one another and with creation were all fundamentally reordered in this *one* man. It was not just Adamic existence that was crucified in Jesus Christ; it was Adam and you and me and the whole human race.

The New Testament is preoccupied with Jesus Christ, the Son of God who became flesh. It wants us to know what became of God, what became of the Son of God. So it narrates the history of the Son for us. He, the eternal Son of God, became human, born of the virgin Mary. He lived. He died. He rose again. He ascended and sits now and forever at the right hand of God the Father almighty. The reason the New Testament is so preoccupied with what became of the Son of God is that it knows that something was becoming of us, the human race, in him. It tells us what became of the Son because it wants us to see what became of the human race in his life and death and resurrection and ascension.

The foundational truth that makes the gospel *good news* to us, without which there is no good news at all, is the connection, the objective union between Jesus Christ and the human race. That connection means that one died for all; therefore all died. That objective union means that the death of Christ was our death; that there and then in Jesus Christ the human race was crucified, dead and buried; that on the Cross of Calvary our disease, our estrangement, our alienation, our flesh, were crucified.

Paul saw it. He saw that Adam's fall and ours, Adam's alienation and ours, Adam's sin and ours, were called to an abrupt end, that there and then in Jesus Christ it was all put to death. And *then* Paul saw the resurrection. If we were united with Jesus Christ in his death, what happened to us in Jesus' resurrection? Listen to what Peter says: "Blessed be the God and Father of our Lord Jesus Christ, who according to His great mercy has caused *us* to be born again to a living hope through the resurrection of Jesus Christ from the dead" (1 Peter 1:3). Jesus Christ died, and Jesus Christ rose again from the dead on Easter Sunday morning. The heart of the gospel is the news that in his death and resurrection, something was happening to you and to me and to the human race. When he died, we died. And when he rose, we rose again to new life, there and then 2000 years ago. Listen to how Paul describes it in Ephesians 2.

> But God, being rich in mercy, because of His great love
> with which He loved us, even when we were dead in our
> transgressions, made us alive together with Christ (by
> grace you have been saved), and raised us up with Him,
> and seated us with Him in the heavenly places in Christ
> Jesus (Ephesians 2:4-6).

The gospel is the astonishing news that something has happened to the Son of God, and the equally astonishing news that in him something has happened to the human race. If the whole human race fell into ruin in Adam—a creature, a mere man—what happened to the human race in the death of Jesus Christ, the incarnate Son of God? Paul tells us. When Jesus Christ died, we died. But that is only the beginning. When he rose, we rose. He ascended and sits at the right hand of God the Father almighty, the place of honor and love and delight and complete and utter acceptance, and Paul tells us that in his ascension we too were lifted up and seated with him at the Father's right hand—and there and then welcomed, accepted, embraced forever.

The gospel is the good news of what became of the Son of God, and of what became of us in him. It is the news that Adam and all of us were crucified with Christ, dead and buried, and on the third day Adam and all of us were quickened with new life and raised with Jesus, and then lifted up to the Father's right hand in Jesus' ascension and seated with Christ.

What happened on the Cross? Why did Jesus die? How do we understand the meaning of his death? The death of Jesus Christ was part of a seamless movement in which the Triune God laid hold of the human race and decisively and sovereignly altered its very existence, cleansing it of all alienation, quickening it with new life and lifting it up into union with the Father, Son and Spirit.

It is finished.

CHAPTER 2

A Note on "Evangelical" Theology

In Jesus Christ, the veil of human mythology was finally and decisively penetrated and the staggering truth about God was fully revealed (Hebrews:1-3). As the early Church wrestled with the revelation of God in Christ, it hammered out the distinctively Christian vision of God as Father, Son and Spirit. Steering a course between errors on the right and on the left, the Church came to understand that the Triune nature of God was not a mere appendix to be attached to an already existing doctrine of God, but a revolutionary insight that was so fundamental it demanded the repentant rethinking of all human conception of God. The relationship of the Father, Son and Spirit is not one truth among other truths about God; it is *the* truth about God. Herein the church and the world find themselves standing before the light of all lights, which not only leads to the true knowledge of God, but also to the true understanding of creation and of human life and history.

Here in Jesus Christ, the human race is summoned before a breathtaking vision of the Triune God and of the eternal passion of the Trinity to bless us beyond our wildest dreams. It is a thrilling and beautiful vision, to be sure, but one that clashes with our natural minds, as Paul says, for the natural mind cannot receive the things of the Spirit (1 Corinthians 2:14). It belongs to the very nature of "revelation" that it commands repentance, a radical change of our basic cast of mind, a complete reorientation of our understanding. For the revelation of God in Christ, beautiful and life-giving as it is, nevertheless cuts against our natural patterns of thought and confronts our mythological projections, our legendary notions of God, of humanity, and of human history.

The Church is called to be the sphere within history where the revelation of God in Christ is allowed to have its way. On the one hand, this means that the Church is called to bring all its notions of God to the bar of revelation to be exposed, evaluated and judged. On the other hand, it means that the Church is called to let the light of Christ be the light which enlightens and leads us step by step into

41

greater and greater clarity. The revelation of God as Father, Son and Spirit calls us to faith and confession, to worship and adoration, to repentance and conversion, and to obedience and faithful thinking, holding forth the promise at every turn that knowing the truth shall set us free with a freedom and life and joy that are beyond this world.

The Legalization of God

In the development of Western theology, things have never been so black and white. The revelation of God in Christ has not been allowed to exercise its proper judgment upon our mythology. Again and again, alien notions of God have been left unchecked—as if the final revelation of God in Christ was only one among several revelations. Foreign ideas about God, ideas which have not been brought before the bar of the Trinity and converted, ideas that may seem obvious and quite plausible to the natural mind, have been allowed to exist side by side with the revelation of God in Christ. These unconverted ideas have not only distorted our understanding of God; they have also shaped our understanding of God's relationship with humanity—with disastrous results.

To begin with, the holiness of God has been given far too prominent a place in our vision of God and of the relationship between God and the human race. Perhaps I speak in haste. For it is not the holiness of God *per se,* but an unconverted view of holiness that has eased its way into the place of prominence in our thinking about God, and shaped virtually everything that has been said about God's relationship with humanity, including Jesus' death on the cross.

In the full and final revelation of God as Father, Son and Spirit, we are given the pair of lenses through which to see the deeper truth of the concepts and ideas that were beginning to take shape in the long history of Israel. As Christians, as those who believe that in Jesus Christ, God has finally broken through the veil of human mythology and revealed the absolute and eternal truth, we are commanded to reread the book, and to rethink all the ideas that were on the road to clarity in Israel. For in Jesus Christ, we are given access to the logic that flows out of the very being of God, and thus to the rhyme and reason that birthed the universe and set human existence on its way.

The holiness of God, the sovereignty and righteousness and justice of God, the love and wrath of God are all essentially Trinitarian concepts. For God did not suddenly become Trinitarian in the time of the New Testament. The God that we meet in Jesus Christ is not a new God. The Triune relationship of Father, Son and Spirit is not a new form that God assumed for a moment in time; it is the way God is from all eternity. But it has taken millennia for God to bring humanity up to speed on the eternal truth. The whole history of Israel, from Genesis to Malachi, constitutes the mere "beginning" of human education. It is at the end of the story, where God finally breaks through human wrongheadedness, that we have the true light by which we can and must interpret everything. Failure here is a failure to be authentically Christian, for it is a failure to take seriously the fact that in Jesus Christ we meet the everlasting truth about God which predates creation and all things.

The holiness of God is one of those special concepts that began to be hammered out in the fallen mind of Israel. Properly understood, the holiness of God is a Trinitarian idea. If we took the joy and the fullness and the love of the Father, Son and Spirit, their mutual delight and passion, the sheer togetherness of their relationship, its intimacy, harmony and wholeness, and rolled them all into one word, it would be "holiness." This one word is pregnant with the wonder and the beauty, the uniqueness and health and rightness of the Trinitarian life.

In the Western tradition, however, the Christian conversion of the idea of holiness, its Trinitarianization, never really developed. Instead, the holiness of God was detached from the Trinity and reconceived within the world of Roman jurisprudence. It was revisioned through Roman concepts of law and order, crime and punishment, blind and cold justice. Reconceived within this stainless steel world of pure law, "holiness" came to mean "legal perfection" or "moral rectitude." This notion of holiness then crept in the back door of the doctrine of God and shaped our entire understanding of God's relationship with humanity and our understanding of the work of Christ itself.

Instead of following through with a Trinitarian understanding of holiness, we allowed the holiness of God to be legalized. The face of God was tarred with the legal brush, so tarred that the fellowship of the Father, Son and Spirit was virtually eclipsed. When that happened, the logic of the universe changed. The framework within which we understand God, creation, and the relationship between God and humanity shifted into an alien legal gear. It became "natural" to think legally, to frame the question of God's relationship with human beings in terms of law and guilt and punishment. But this line of thought betrays the fact that there is something much more ancient about God's relationship with human beings than the law.

Before there was ever any law, there was the Trinity and the irrepressible life and fellowship and joy of the Triune God. The logic of the universe and of human existence flows out of this relationship. The eternal purpose of this Triune God is not to place us under law and turn us into religious legalists, but to include us in their relationship, to give us a place in their shared life and fellowship and joy. If we must speak in terms of law, then we must say that the law of this universe is the primal decision of the Father, Son and Spirit to give humanity a place in the Trinitarian life. This eternal purpose to adopt humanity, to include us in the Trinitarian circle, predates all things and is the proper framework, or the logic, within which we are to understand creation, the Fall of Adam, Israel, the coming of Jesus Christ and his death, resurrection and ascension.

Everything that the Triune God does, from creation to shouting the intolerable "No!" in the teeth of the Fall, from the calling of Israel to the death and resurrection and ascension of Jesus, flows out of and serves the one eternal purpose of the Father, Son and Spirit to include humanity in the Trinitarian circle. There is no other God and no other will of God for humanity. The union forged in Jesus, the exaltation of humanity in him to the right hand of God, is not a divine afterthought; it is the eternal foreword, the one Word of God from the beginning. To put this in St. Paul's language, the Father predestined us to adoption through Jesus Christ before the foundation of the world (Ephesians 1:5). This will for our adoption, this will for our inclusion in the circle of life shared by the Father, Son and Spirit, precedes all things and stands as the one driving passion of all divine activity. And it stands as the true logic in and through which we are bound to interpret the universe and human existence within it. Jesus Christ is, as he says, the light of the world (John 8:12).

The Eclipse of the Gospel

The Western tradition, and within it, modern evangelical theology, translated God and God's relationship with human beings through the meat grinder of legal categories. In doing so, it lost meaningful touch with the Trinity and the eternal purpose of the Triune God. A legal notion of holiness infiltrated the doctrine of God and rewrote the logic of God's relationship with humanity. The Fall of Adam, the calling of Israel, and the person and work of Jesus Christ, especially his death on the cross, were all then perceived through this alien legal logic. Legal holiness, law and justice, guilt and punishment figured as the supreme hermeneutical law through which even God was interpreted—or reinterpreted. This was a fundamental error and the chief sin of Western Christianity, out of which all manner of disaster has come. The price tag on such a blunder is an unspeakably perverse vision of God that is now etched into the psyche of the Western mind, a perverse vision that not only fuels our ingrained anxiety, but produces empty religion that wears us out and bores us with the idea of the "gospel" itself, and leaves us more hopeless than ever.

The gospel typically preached by modern evangelicals begins with the statement that God is holy (holy in the legal sense). The human race has fallen into sin and is guilty before God. Since God is holy, He cannot allow sin to go unpunished—justice requires punishment. But since God is also loving, He sends Jesus Christ to take our place. On the cross, the guilt of the human race is placed upon Jesus Christ, and Jesus suffers the just punishment for our guilt. The cry of Jesus, "My God, My God, why have You forsaken me?" is interpreted as the moment of moments when the Father, being too holy to look upon evil, turns His back upon His Son in utter abandonment. The Father forsakes His Son. That forsakenness, that abandonment and its unsearchable agony, is then interpreted as the punishment for our sins that satisfies God's justice—in this legal or Evangelical model.

The first disaster of this interpretation is that the work of Jesus Christ is turned on its head. The New Testament nowhere says that *God* was being reconciled in the work of Jesus; it says that God was in Christ reconciling *the world* to Himself (2 Corinthians 5:18-19).

45

As Paul insists, it was while we were utterly helpless, while we were sinners who had sold ourselves irretrievably into bondage and unwittingly set ourselves in opposition to God, that God acted to save us (Romans 5:6-10). But here, in the legal model, the order has been reversed, such that Jesus has come to save us not from ourselves and the catastrophe of Adam, but from God. Changing God has become the object of Christ's work. If we ask the question, "Why did Jesus die?" then the answer that flows out of the legal framework is that he died so that God the Father would be different. Whereas the Trinitarian understanding sees Jesus sent by the Father to convert fallen Adamic existence to Himself, the legal model leaves us with a Jesus who comes to convert God! In the legal view, the result of the death of Jesus Christ is a fundamental change in God's attitude towards humanity and in His relationship with us. The Father, not fallen humanity, is what gets altered on the cross, in the legal view.

The clear message imbedded in the way the legal view frames the gospel is that there is a side of God that is not "for us" at all, a side that needs to be changed, that needs to be conditioned into being gracious, a side that needs to be converted. When we give the Trinity its proper place in our thinking, however, we see clearly that God is eternally "for us," and thus that there is no part of God that needs to be changed or converted or conditioned. Before the foundation of the world, the Father, Son and Spirit set their determined love upon us and set their hand to the plow to bring us into the circle of their shared life. This purpose stands. Adam's sin did not alter God or God's purpose in any way. The Fall constitutes a problem, to be sure. For in the Fall the human race, which God has determined to bring to glory, became corrupt, estranged, fundamentally alien to God. Thus the problem, from the Trinitarian perspective, is that the human race stands in need of a radical conversion to God. Punishment has never been the point. It has never crossed God's mind, and even if it did, it would not do a thing to overcome the real problem of our estrangement and so fulfill God's purpose and dreams for us. The Father's passion is to get His children back and to bless us with all the treasures of heaven itself. Unto that end the Son was sent into our existence to undo *our* estrangement, not God's, and to convert our fallen human existence to God. This love of God in action, this agonizing incarnation suffering to convert humanity, is the wrath of God, the fiery and complete opposition of God's love to our destruction.

The second disaster of the legal interpretation is that it leaves us with a God divided into two opposing parts. Instead of seeing God as Father, Son and Spirit and seeing that the love, mercy and grace of God, as well as the holiness and justice and wrath of God, are all expressions of the fellowship of the Trinity, and of the single-minded devotion of the Triune God to us, the legal model forces us to think of God as divided. The legal message drives a wedge between the love of God and the holiness of God. On the one side, there is the love of God, and with this love, His mercy and grace. On the other side, there is the holiness of God, and with this holiness, His justice and wrath. Whereas the one side of God loves us, that love "cannot" accept us until the other side is "satisfied" by proper suffering. It is as if there are two wills of God vying for control of God's relationship with the human race. Are we to believe that the Father has such a division within Him, such a split personality? Are we to conclude that the loving side of the Father sends the Son to suffer the punishment demanded by the holy side of the Father, so that the Father can then be whole, single-minded towards us! Are we to believe that only one side of God sends Jesus to save? Are we to believe that Jesus Christ heals the Father's split personality and brings Him into one mind towards us? Does Jesus actually make the Father whole?

Jesus Christ is the revelation of God, not of a part of God or of one side of God, but of the very being and character of God. What we see in Jesus is that the Father has never once forsaken us or even considered such a thing. Jesus is the proof that the Father's love is utterly unwavering and that His eternal dreams for us stand. The Son was sent by the Father to find us. He was sent as the living expression of the fire of love in the Father's belly, as the enactment of the eternal Word of God to have us as His beloved children, and he was sent to search us out in the far country, to cleanse us of all alienation and bring us home at all costs. For the Father will have it no other way. If we must speak of the death of Jesus Christ as "satisfaction," we must see that what is satisfied in his death is the Father's utterly single-minded devotion to us and His relentless determination that His extravagant plans for us would be fulfilled—even at the cost of His own beloved Son's life.

When the doctrine of God is legalized, we end up with a perverse vision of the Father who is of two minds about us. One side of the Father loves us, while the other side couldn't care less; in fact, the other side could not possibly tolerate such love and certainly could not allow it to embrace us and accept us freely. This leaves us with a Jesus who comes to suffer the punishment required by his Father's holiness so that the hands of the Father's love can at last be untied and He is free to embrace us.

This picture, already horrendous and destructive enough, is plunged into greater darkness when wrongheaded notions of wrath are added. If we put this scenario into the language of Jonathan Edwards' famous sermon, "Sinners in the Hands of an Angry God," then that moment of moments when Jesus Christ takes upon himself our sin is the moment when he suffers not merely justice or the consequences of sin, but *anger.* The holy God who requires strict justice, on the legal model, is now translated into an angry executioner who demands that His anger be spent.

Edwards' notion of the profoundly angry God pushes the problem from God "cannot," to God "will not," accept us. It is not simply a matter of holiness requiring sufficient punishment before forgiveness can be allowed; it is now a matter of God breathing fire and spitting nails and demanding that His brooding vengeance be vented and His untold righteous anger be satisfied.

> The bow of God's wrath is bent, and the arrow made ready
> on the string, and justice bends the arrow at your heart, and
> strains the bow, and it is nothing but the mere pleasure of
> God, and that of an angry God, without any promise or
> obligation at all, that keeps the arrow one moment from
> being made drunk with your blood.[9]

Edwards' picture of God is a long way from the God of Athanasius and the Nicene Creed. Note the contrast in the spirit and in the vision of the character of God:

> It was unworthy of the goodness of God that creatures
> made by Him should be brought to nothing through the

---

[9] "Sinners in the Hands of an Angry God" in *The Works of Jonathan Edwards* [Edinburgh: Banner of Truth Trust] Vol. 2, p. 9.

deceit wrought upon man by the devil; and it was supremely unfitting that the work of God in mankind should disappear, either through their own negligence or through the deceit of evil spirits. As, then, the creatures whom He had created....were on the road to ruin, what then was God, being Good, to do? Was He to let corruption and death have their way with them? In that case, what was the use of having made them in the beginning? Surely it would have been better never to have been created at all than, having been created, to be neglected and perish; and, besides that, such indifference to the ruin of His own work before His very eyes would argue not goodness in God but limitation.... It was impossible, therefore, that God should leave man to be carried off by corruption, because it would be unfitting and unworthy of Himself.[10]

For Athanasius, it is unthinkable that God would turn his back upon His creation. The work of God in creation flows out of the endless love of the Father, Son and Spirit. If God were suddenly to turn cold towards the human race, such a turn would indicate that coldness, indifference or neutrality is part of the relationship of the Triune God—or else that God is suddenly acting contrary to the way the Father, Son and Spirit have existed from all eternity.

In Athanasius, the Fall of Adam is met by the same God and by the same overflowing love and determination to bless that called forth creation in the first place. The passion of God in creation becomes the fire that sends the Son to save. It is God's dreams for us that are threatened in Adam's plunge. For Edwards, on the other hand, the Fall of Adam is met by cold justice, so cold that it is heartlessly unmoved by the destruction of humanity. The God of Edward's sermon couldn't care less about His own creation. In His heart, indifferent and arbitrary as it is, there is no compelling reason to act for the salvation of His creation at all. The passionate love that Athanasius sees everywhere, especially in response to the Fall, is strangely absent in Edwards. In its place we have pure anger.

The legalization of God reaches its purest expression right here in the unmoved indignation of Edward's God, a God who cannot

---

[10] *St. Athanasius on the Incarnation: The Treatise De Incarnatione Verbi Dei,* translated and edited by a Religious of C. S. M. V. (London: A. R. Mowbray & Co.) § 6.

accept us and is not interested in even considering such a thing. Until the arrow has struck its mark and is drunk with blood, the vengeance, the fiery wrath of the legalized God, remains unrelieved. And until that wrath is vented and appeased, there is no possibility that this God will accept guilty sinners, or even consider it. Legal justice is one thing; divine anger is quite another. Jesus Christ, in this scenario, goes to the cross not to undo the Fall of Adam and bring us to his Father, or even to suffer the consequences of our sin; he goes to the cross to suffer the anger, the holy rage, of God the Father.

To make the point, as the punishment theorists are quick to do, that the Father sends the Son out of His love for sinners only confirms the dreadful split in the personality of the Father. For strictly speaking, it is not the Father who sends the Son, on this model; it is *one side* of the Father. The loving side of the Father sends the Son, while the holy side of the Father is not in the least interested in such mercy; indeed, the dark side of God is utterly opposed to such a gratuitous action.

This perverse split in the Father, however, is not even the worst part of this picture. For the legalization of God shreds the unity of the Trinity itself. How is it that the Father has eyes too holy to look upon sin, yet the Son not only looks at sin, he takes it upon himself; indeed, in Paul's mind, he becomes sin? (2 Corinthians 5:21). How can the Father be holier than the Son? How can they be in two opposing minds about sin? How can the Trinity be so divided and the Father and Son so fundamentally different? How can the Father's blood boil with such anger and be so bent on retribution, when there is no trace of such feeling in Jesus Christ?

The question here is whether or not Jesus Christ is God. Is it true that to see Jesus is to see the Father? Or is Jesus the revelation of only one side of God? Is there another side of God behind the back of Christ, a side that Jesus does not reveal at all, and in fact comes to change? Has Edwards, and by implication much of what passes as evangelical theology, not betrayed Jesus Christ here, theologically speaking? Has he not failed to take the deity of Christ seriously when it comes to thinking out his vision of God? What is the origin of this God of unmoved indignation? Is it Jesus? *Christ alone* is as much a statement about how Christians are to think faithfully about God as it is a statement about the way of our justification.

What we learn in Jesus Christ is that God is Father, Son and Spirit. We see this relationship—its wholeness and rightness and goodness, its unity and love and fellowship, and its wrath—lived out in the pages of the New Testament. It is our Christian duty, and the highest of all privileges, to reread the book in this light and to rethink everything in the universe, including what we think we know about God, in sheer faithfulness to the full and final revelation given in Jesus Christ. Anything less is neither Christian nor Evangelical.

The Legacy of the Legalized God

On the practical side of things, the legalization of God has left a legacy of devastation at the soul level. To begin with, the legal model sets before us a gospel that is powerless to produce assurance. How is it possible for human beings to experience even a modicum of assurance when God is so divided, so double-minded? Whatever assurance may arise in our hearts when we hear of the love of God in Jesus Christ is immediately poisoned when we hear that this love flows out of only one side of God. Even if we do not buy into Edwards' picture of the angry archer, the legal model still leaves us with a God of ambiguity towards the human race. The framing of the gospel itself, in the legal model, teaches us that there is a side of God that does not like us at all, a side that would just as soon have us miserable and broken and enslaved to darkness as it would to see us whole and complete and living in joy. Such ambiguity on the face of God does not heal the lethal roux simmering in our souls; it fuels it.

The legal gospel, with its double-minded God, is incapable of producing peace, real hope, and abiding assurance in the human soul. It is incapable of producing the rest for our souls that Jesus promised. It is one thing to be riddled with anxiety because we are in the dark about the heart of God towards us; it is quite another when the "gospel" tells us that God's heart itself is divided toward us, and thus that there is every reason to be anxious. Far from bringing relief, such a message leaves the human race more afraid, more insecure than ever, and it leaves the Church hiding from the Father behind the blood of Jesus. The legacy of the legalized God is not life in the baptism of assurance, with its joy and freedom; it is life in anxiety, with

51

the unspoken prayer that the other side of God will remain quiet.

Is it any wonder that the joy of the Church is so insipid these days, so very much like the "joy" of the unbeliever? Do we not all suffer from the same distorted vision of God? Assurance is not a peripheral luxury; it is the heart and soul of Christian living. Without assurance, we will never experience freedom from our entrenched self-centeredness, freedom to go out of ourselves and give ourselves to others. Without assurance, we will never experience freedom to know and be known. Without that freedom, we will never know real fellowship, and without fellowship we will never experience the unspeakable joy of our adoption in Jesus Christ. What kind of Christian life does that leave us living? As long as the legalized vision of God is etched into the psyche of the Church, the Church is doomed to live in the same bondage as the unbeliever. For the wages of legalism are the same as the wages of darkness—anxiety, fear and insecurity. There is no baptism of assurance when God is so double-minded. Without that baptism, our profound anxiety is unrelieved and our self-centeredness is unhealed.

In the strangest of ironies, the legalized God actually drives us away from Jesus Christ, at least one side of us. The fiery wrath of the legalized God may (or may not) be satisfied in Jesus, but we are still corrupt, still diseased, still afflicted by the baptism of anxiety. Jesus has successfully changed God, on the legal model, but he has left the human race broken. And worse, we are left to ourselves to find healing. For Jesus has not dealt with our estrangement, at least not within this framework. How then will we find any real healing? Where do we turn for *our* conversion? The irony here is that for all of its focus upon Jesus Christ, the legalized version of the gospel ends up driving us away from Christ to find *our* conversion somewhere else. Faith in Jesus Christ may get God reconciled to us, but it leaves us in our disease, and thus inevitably launches us into a search for a second work of salvation beyond Jesus Christ, a search for something that can do for us what he could not and did not do.

We love Jesus, to be sure, but we are torn, for part of us knows by experience that this Jesus is not much help in the real world of marriage, family and relationships, of work and play and social justice—not much help in the business of *life*. So we raise one hand in worship of Jesus, while we feel around with the other to find something beyond him that can heal our souls and bring healing to our actual lives—to our boring marriages and family problems, to our depression and mental illness. This searching is what keeps the self-help authors in business, as well as the second-blessing pundits and a great many preachers and churches.

The legal model leaves us with one eye on Jesus and one eye scanning the horizon for the next thing to come along that promises relief—a new religious program, a new technique to charm the Spirit into blessing, a new formula for successful Christian living—all of which sends us running around the hamster's wheel until we eventually drop in sheer exhaustion. Far from filling us with unbounded hope and delivering our souls from fear, so that our relationships can begin to be whole and real and beautiful, the legal gospel turns us in upon ourselves. It forces us into repression, into hiding and self-protection, such that our soul issues are never addressed and never healed. The staggering truth of who we are in Jesus Christ is chained and cannot get loose to express itself in self-giving love, in fellowship, in the untold joy of our adoption in Christ. What kind of Christian life does that leave us living? Why would the watching world be interested in anything we have to say?

The ineffectiveness of the legal gospel to touch our real lives and the things that we care most about as human beings has left the Western world utterly bored with the idea of Christianity, so bored that it is well-nigh impossible for us to give Jesus serious attention. The legacy of the legalized God is anxiety, and that means self-centeredness, and self-centeredness means broken marriages and failed relationships; it means baseball teams that are dominated by coaches who justify their existence by the good works of their players' performance; it means parents who cannot let their children play and children who cannot believe that their parents understand life. Self-centeredness transforms our lives into a long and frantic attempt to save ourselves, to create legendary lives that will at least hint at wholeness. It produces a culture that looks like a disturbed ant bed, a culture that eventually leaves us worn out and sad and empty and headed for the nearest pub. All the while, an utterly glorious day—filled with staggering beauty and irrepressible joy—has been created for us by the overflowing philanthropy of the Triune God.

The Truth Again

The life that God lives as Father, Son and Spirit is not boring and sad and lonely. There is no emptiness in this circle, no depression or fear or angst. The Trinitarian life is a life of unchained fellowship and intimacy, fired by passionate, self-giving love and mutual delight. Such love, giving rise to such togetherness and fellowship, overflows in unbounded joy, in infinite creativity and unimaginable goodness. The gospel begins here with this God and with this divine life, for there is no other. Before time dawned and space was called to be, before the heavens were stretched out and filled with a sea of stars, before the earth was summoned and filled with people and life and endless beauty, before there was anything, there was the Father, Son and Spirit and the great dance of Trinitarian life. The amazing truth is that this Triune God, in staggering and lavish love, determined to open the circle and share the Trinitarian life with others. This is the one, eternal and abiding reason for the existence of the universe and human life within it. There is no other God, no other will of God, no second plan, no hidden agenda for human beings. From the beginning, God is Father, Son and Spirit, and from the beginning, this God has determined not to exist without us.

In the event of Adam's Fall and the sheer disaster it sent rippling through God's creation, the one will of the Triune God held fast. The catastrophe of Adam ran into the same passionate and determined love that birthed creation in the beginning, and therefore into an intolerable divine "No!" The Father, Son and Spirit were opposed, passionately and utterly opposed, to our destruction and immediately began the work of reconciliation. In fact, Jesus Christ was on the road to the incarnation while Adam was a mere thought in the mind of God. For there could not possibly be a union between God and humanity except through a staggering act of stooping on God's part. Before creation, our adoption—and its accomplishment in Jesus Christ—was raised as the banner of all banners in heaven.

It was not the Fall of Adam, therefore, that set God's agenda; it was the decision to share the great dance with us through Jesus. Adam's plunge certainly threatened God's dreams for us, but that threat had been anticipated and already strategically overcome in the predestination of the incarnation. Jesus Christ did not become human to fix the Fall; he became human to accomplish the eternal purpose of our adoption, and in order to bring our adoption to pass, the Fall had to be called to a halt and undone. The catastrophe of Adam certainly made the road of incarnation, and thus of our adoption, one of pain and suffering and death, but it did not create its necessity. Jesus is not a footnote to Adam and his Fall; the Fall, and indeed creation itself, is a footnote to the purpose of God in Jesus Christ.

In the teeth of Adam's plunge, Abraham and Israel were called to be the sphere within the lost world of Adam where the one will of God could continue unfolding and the womb for the incarnation could be prepared. In the fullness of time, the Son of God was sent by the Father into the far country of fallen Adamic existence. There, born into Adam's darkness and into Israel's fiery conflict with God, he stepped into human history—and thus into the violent contradiction between fallen humanity and the Triune God. There, inside Adam's skin but refusing to live in Adam's mythology, he took his stand as the Father's beloved Son, steadfastly loving his Father with all of his heart, soul, mind and strength and sharing all things with Him in the fellowship of the Spirit. He bore the contradiction in himself and resolved it through 33 years of fire and trial and suffering, walking not in the way of Adam but in the way of the true Son. He penetrated to the core of human estrangement and alienation and experienced it fully, but did so as the One who knows and loves the Father, thus denying his Adamic flesh and crucifying it on the cross of Calvary, and therefore healing the terrible breach between God and lost humanity in himself. What emerges on the other side of the cross is a human being from the lost world of Adam who sits at the Father's right hand in real and abiding fellowship with Him. Jesus has not only overcome the Fall of Adam; he has exalted human existence into the circle of the Trinitarian life of God, and fulfilled the eternal purpose of the Triune God for us.

The very essence of the gospel lies right here in Jesus Christ himself, in his humanity, in his incarnate relationship with the Father in the Spirit, and in the mysterious way in which he included us in this relationship. For the great conversion of his humanity to his Father, wrought out through 33 years of fire and trial, and decisively accomplished in his death and resurrection, was a vicarious event. The miraculous and wonderful truth is that we were included in his baptism, in his life and death, in his resurrection and ascension. When he died, we died. When he rose, we rose. When he ascended to the Father, he took the whole human race with him to the right hand of God the Father almighty—inside the circle of all circles, into the very life of the Triune God. With this, and this alone, the Father is at last thrilled, for our exaltation and adoption in Jesus Christ is the fulfillment of the primal decision made before all worlds began.

Upon the homecoming of the incarnate Son, with the human race gathered in his arms, the Spirit of adoption was unleashed upon the world with the singular mission of leading us to *know* the truth. The Spirit was sent to testify of Christ, to bear witness with our spirits that we *are* children of God in Jesus, and in bearing witness, to call us to believe the truth so that we can experience its liberation. The Spirit testifies of Jesus Christ as the Father's beloved Son, who sits at His right hand, and to Jesus Christ as the Lord and Saviour of the human race, who has searched the universe for us, found us and taken us home. As he leads us to know the truth, not just in our heads as a bit of theological trivia, but in our souls as the surest thing in all the world, he brings us into the baptism of assurance. For to see ourselves seated with Christ at the Father's right hand, to see ourselves loved and cherished, embraced and accepted by the Father, delighted in, is to know untold relief and hope and peace, and the deepest and dearest of all assurances. Such assurance, in turn, begins to war against our ingrained anxiety and to deliver us from its stepchild, self-centerednesss. We become free to go out of ourselves, to notice others and to care for them, free to know and be known, to love, and thus free to experience real fellowship. And in such fellowship, the very life of the Triune God, the great dance of life shared by the Father, Son and Spirit, is released in our lives.

It is to be emphasized that Jesus Christ did not change God the Father, and neither does our faith. Before the creation of the world, the Father, Son and Spirit set their lavish and determined love upon us and have never wavered. Out of that eternal love, Jesus was sent to find us in the far country, to lay hold of us, cleanse us of all alienation and bring us to his Father. On the heels of Christ's accomplishment, and out of the same eternal love, the Spirit was poured out upon us to lead us to know the truth—the truth about God and humanity in Jesus Christ—so that we can experience its liberation and life.

Our faith does not alter God in the least. Faith is first and foremost a discovery of the heart of the Father, Son and Spirit, a discovery of the astonishing dreams of the Triune God for our blessing, and of the fact that those dreams have now become eternal truth in Jesus Christ. Such a discovery cannot help but take our breath away and fill our hearts with hope and peace and assurance. The Spirit's witness, when believed, produces the fruit of the Spirit in our lives. Living water flowing out of our innermost beings into our relationships, our work and play. Faith does not change God; it changes *us*. It delivers us from our mythology and its spiritual agony—and from the way this spiritual agony poisons our lives. Without faith in Jesus Christ, our souls—and thus our relationships, our work and play—are already afflicted with anxiety. The only cure in the universe is to see Jesus Christ seated at the Father's right hand and ourselves seated with him. The discovery of this truth commands faith, for it gives us something to believe in, something that is so real, so solid and true that to believe it baptizes our anxious souls with assurance, the most liberating force in all the earth.

CHAPTER 3

A Note on "My God, My God,
Why Have You Forsaken Me?"

Psalm 22:1 begins with the most haunting cry in the Bible: "My God, My God, why have You forsaken me?" Both Matthew and Mark tell us that Jesus took up this cry when he was dying on the cross. It is very natural for us, steeped as we are in the Western framework, with its fundamental legal orientation, to see this cry of Jesus as the supreme expression of his suffering. With the dark side of the Father in the background, the Son takes upon himself our sin and the Father unleashes the fury of His eternal wrath upon His own Son. In that horrible, unspeakable moment, Jesus cries out, "My God, My God, why have You forsaken me?"

Why is it that we are so prone to zero in on this statement of Jesus from the cross? There are other statements from Jesus in that hour; why does this one get so much press? Why not focus on "It is finished" or "Father into your hands I commend my spirit"? Is it an exaggeration to say that more ink has been spilled on "My God, My God, why have you forsaken me?" than on all the other statements of Jesus from the cross put together? It should come as no surprise if it is true, for that is where we are led when we lose meaningful contact with the Trinity and the eternal purpose of the Triune God for us. We are left with a legalized God of holy anger, and we find our only hope on the cross where Jesus suffers God's vengeance in our place. Such a verse naturally speaks volumes to us.

Is this the correct interpretation of this verse? What if we read it as true Christians, with the Triune God, not the legalized God of holy anger, in the back of our minds?

This cry of Jesus is a direct quotation from Psalm 22. If we read the Psalm as a whole, we find the message does not end in despair at all, but victory. It ends with the remarkable prophecy:

> All the ends of the earth will remember and turn to the Lord, and all the families of the nations will worship before Thee.....They will come and will declare His right-

eousness to a people who will be born, that He has performed it (vv. 27 & 31).

Between that cry and that prophecy lies the whole range of human emotion. The first two verses are words of deep despair: "My God, My God, why have You forsaken me? ...O my God, I cry by day, but You do not answer." The anguish of the Psalmist is heightened by the fact that his cries to God are met with stone-cold silence. But in his despair, he rehearses the faith of his fathers. He goes back to the old stories of God's faithfulness: "In You our fathers trusted; they trusted and You delivered them. To You they cried out and were delivered. In You they trusted and were not disappointed" (vv.4-5).

But then the Psalmist takes a turn into deeper darkness: "But *I* am a worm, and not a man. A reproach of men, and despised by the people" (v. 6). He is well aware of the faithfulness of God to the heroes of the faith, but I, he thinks to himself, am no hero. I am not even a good person. Even the people despise me. They mock my trust in God. Go ahead, they say, commit yourself to the Lord and see what happens. Let the Lord deliver *you.*

Who can stand before God and claim that God ought to be faithful to him because of his own faithfulness to God? The minute we turn in upon ourselves as the basis of God's faithfulness to us, is the minute our despair becomes utterly overwhelming. But again, the Psalmist makes an abrupt turn. He looks away from himself and from the mocking of the people back to God. "Yet," he says, "You are the One who brought me forth from the womb. You made me trust when I was at my mother's breast. Upon You I was cast from birth and You have been my God from my mother's womb" (vv. 9-10). Then the Psalmist cries out to God for deliverance.

> Be not far from me, for trouble is near and there is none to help. Many bulls have surrounded me, strong bulls of Bashan have encircled me. They open wide their mouth at me, as a ravening and roaring lion. I am poured out like water. All my bones are out of joint. My heart is like wax. It is melted within me. My strength is dried up like a potsherd, and my tongue cleaves to my jaws. And you have laid me in the dust of death. For dogs have surrounded me. A band of evildoers has encompassed me. They

> pierced my hands and my feet. I can count all my bones. They look, they stare at me. They divide my garments among them, and cast lots for my clothing.
>
> But You, O Lord, be not far off. O Lord my help, hasten to my assistance. Deliver my soul from the sword. My only life from the power of the dog. Save me from the lion's mouth, and from the horns of the wild oxen answer me (vv. 11-21).

The trauma of the Psalmist is overwhelming. The dogs, the wild beasts, the roaring lions have surrounded him and are ready to pounce for the kill. His insides are shredded with fear. He has no courage and no hope. He cries out to God for deliverance.

Then the Psalm makes another turn. The despair ends and the praise begins and the whole ordeal comes to a victorious end, such that coming generations will look back upon this event and see that the Lord has performed His salvation.

> I will tell of Your name to my brethren. In the midst of the assembly I will praise You.... For He has not despised nor abhorred the affliction of the afflicted. Neither has He hidden His face from him; but when he cried to Him for help, He heard (vv. 22, 24).
>
> From You comes my praise in the great assembly.... All the ends of the earth will remember and turn to the Lord, and all the families of the nations will worship before You. For the kingdom is the Lord's, and He rules over the nations.... Posterity will serve Him. It will be told of the Lord to the coming generation. They will come and will declare His righteousness to a people who will be born, that He has performed it (vv. 25, 27-31).

Psalm 22 moves from agony to God's victorious intervention and to a prophecy that the coming generations will look back upon this moment as the salvation of the Lord of Hosts.

Why did Jesus quote the opening verse of this Psalm? In his day, to hear the first verse of a Psalm was like hearing the beginning of the tune of a favorite song. The tune jump-starts the tape in our heads and sends us singing the rest of the song. I suspect that when Jesus quoted the first line of Psalm 22, he was jump-starting the memory of the whole Psalm in the minds of the people around him. For they all knew it by heart. In doing so, he was interpreting the event of his suffering and death for them. He was telling them what was happening.

On the cross, Jesus surely identified with the suffering of the Psalmist, but he also identified with the whole Psalm. What is happening on the Cross? What is the meaning of this event? Jesus is answering all these questions. He is saying, 'Here it is, right here in Psalm 22.' It looks as though all is lost. It looks as though the dogs are winning and as if God has abandoned me, utterly forsaken me to the abyss. But this is not the case. "For He has *not* despised nor abhorred the affliction of the afflicted; neither has He *hidden His face* from him" (v. 24). Indeed, the very opposite is the truth, and all the world will come to know it as the Lord's salvation.

In the greatest of ironies, the cry of Jesus, "My God, My God, why have You forsaken me?" actually sets in motion a line of thought that completely reinterprets what is happening on the cross. Far from being a perverse moment when the angry God pours His wrath out upon the Son and utterly rejects him, the cross is the moment when the Father absolutely refuses to forsake His Son, the moment of moments when He does not hide His face, or turn His back upon him in disgust. Here, according to the Psalm and its interpretation of the event, there is no forsaking at all. In fact, the Psalm tells us that the coming generations will see this event not as divine rejection, but precisely as divine presence and rescue and salvation.

Is it accidental that the Spirit has so directed things that Psalm 22 is followed by the great Shepherd Psalm? What if we were to read on from Psalm 22 into Psalm 23? What would we find?

> The Lord is my shepherd, I shall not want. He makes me lie down in green pastures. He leads me beside quiet waters. He restores my soul. He guides me in the paths of righteousness for His name's sake. *Even though I walk through the valley of the shadow of death, I fear no evil, for You are with me.* Your rod and Your staff, they comfort me. You prepare a table before me in the presence of my enemies. You anoint my head with oil. My cup overflows. Surely goodness and loving-kindness will follow me all

the days of my life, and *I will dwell in the house of the Lord forever.*

Far from being a moment when the wrath of God is vented upon the Son, the cross is the moment when the relationship of the Father and Son is most triumphant in the greatest darkness. On the cross, Jesus penetrated to the core of Adamic estrangement, where everything shouts that God has rejected us and abandoned us to the abyss. But it was precisely there, precisely in the experience of that estrangement and horror, that the fellowship of the Father and Son and Spirit stood fast. Even though I walk through the valley of *the shadow of death,* I fear no evil, *for You are with me.*

And suppose we read on from Psalm 23 into Psalm 24 and to that magnificent shout:

> Lift up your heads, O gates. And be lifted up, O ancient doors. That the King of glory may come in! (24: 7).

If we take these three Psalms together, we are face to face not only with the sufferings of Jesus on the cross, but also with his resurrection and ascension. We are confronted with the fact that the relationship between the Father and Son in the Spirit, far from being ripped apart, held fast through the deepest of human despair. There is no forsaking by the Father. Even when Jesus walked through the valley of the shadow of death, the Father did not forsake him; He *saved* him. On the other side of that valley, the Father and Son are still together, and we stand before the vision of the gates of Heaven itself opening in triumph and celebration before the homecoming of the Father's Son. Lift up your heads, O gates, for the Son of the Father is coming home—and he has the whole human race with him.

> "They will come and will declare His righteousness to a people who will be born, that He has performed it."

CHAPTER 4

A Good Friday Sermon: On the Death
of Our Blessed Lord Jesus Christ

Hebrews 1:1-3

The question confronting us in this hour is the question *Why?*
Why did Jesus Christ die? Why was it necessary? Why did it have
to happen? And with this question others follow. What happened in
Jesus' death? How do we understand the sufferings of Jesus? How
do we understand what happened in this, the darkest hour in the history of the cosmos?

There is a part of me that says it is best not to venture forth here.
Standing before such a profound event as the death of Jesus Christ,
we should simply cover our mouths in absolute silence. For who are
we to speak about such a matter? But there is another part of me that
asks how we can possibly be silent, when ignorance of such glorious
truth leaves us in bondage. How can we be silent when such errors
abound about our blessed Lord's death, and when these errors leave a
trail of human wreckage behind them? We are forced, as St. Hilary
said, "to deal with unlawful matters, to scale perilous heights, to
speak unutterable words, and to trespass forbidden ground," and to
"strain the poor resources of our language to express thoughts too
great for words.[11] And so we pray with Hilary for "precision of language, soundness of argument, grace of style, loyalty to truth."[12]

Why did Jesus Christ die? What happened in his death? The
answer to these questions is found in three words, and in what these
three words represent.

The first word is *Trinity.* If we are to understand why Jesus Christ
died, we must go all the way back to the beginning, indeed to before
the beginning. We must go back before creation to the Creator who
called forth the universe in the first place. For the way we understand
God–His being and character and heart–decisively shapes the way we
answer the questions, "Why did Jesus die, and what happened in his
death?"

---

[11] Hilary, *De Trinitate,* II.2.
[12] Hilary, *De Trinitate,* I.37.

As the early Church was forced, on the one hand, to wrestle with those who denied the deity of our blessed Lord Jesus Christ, and on the other with those who said that God is alone and solitary and merely changes faces, the Church hammered out the Christian vision of God as Holy Trinity, and took its stand. The early Church came to know that the relationship between the Father, Son and Spirit we see lived out on the pages of the New Testament was not a mere form that God assumed for a moment in time, but *the* eternal truth about God. God *is* and always has been and always will be Father, Son and Spirit.

When we confess the Nicene Creed and affirm that Jesus Christ is the *eternal* Son of God, we are saying with St. Athanasius and the whole Church that there was never a time when God was alone, when the Father was not Father, and the Son and the Spirit were not present. There was never a time when there was just God, so to speak, just some abstract omni-being, some great, nameless unmoved mover, some faceless force up there somewhere. From all eternity, God is Father, Son and Spirit, and this means that God is fundamentally a relational being. This means that fellowship and togetherness, camaraderie and communion have always been at the center of the being of God and always will be. It is critical that you see this. And it is just as critical that you see that the shared life of the Father, Son and Spirit is not boring or sad or lonely. There is no emptiness in this circle, no depression or fear or anxiety. The Trinitarian life is a life of unchained fellowship and intimacy, fired by passionate, self-giving love and mutual delight. Such passionate love, giving rise to such free-flowing fellowship and togetherness, overflows in unbounded joy, in infinite creativity and in inconceivable goodness.

If we are to understand why Jesus Christ died, we must begin with who God is, and therefore we begin with the Holy Trinity and with the abounding and glorious and rich and overflowing fellowship of the Father, Son and Spirit. For *this Triune God* is the Creator, and this divine life of togetherness and communion is the womb of creation, and this divine fellowship of unbounded joy is the rhyme and reason behind the existence of the human race and of every person within it. There is no other god.

The second word that answers why Jesus Christ died and what happened in his death is the word *ascension.* At this very hour, a *man* sits at the right hand of God the Father almighty. At this moment, a *human being* lives and dwells and abides inside the circle of all circles, inside everything that it means to be God, inside the very life and fellowship of the Father, Son and Spirit. "On the third day he rose again from the dead according to the Scriptures, and ascended into heaven and sitteth at the right hand of the Father," as the Creed says.

There is no more stunning news in the universe than the news that a human being now exists inside the Trinitarian life of God. It was not an angel or a ghost that St. Stephen saw standing at the right hand of God in heaven. It was *Jesus.* It was the *incarnate* Son. What could be more astonishing than the news that the very communion of the Triune God has opened itself up, and that it now and forever includes a human being within it? Do you see that? Of all the things that we read about in the Bible, the most astonishing, the most shocking, the most mind-boggling is the ascension of the man Jesus, the *incarnate* Son.

Now let me ask another question. Was the ascension of the incarnate Son an accident? Is the fact that now and forever a *human being,* Jesus Christ, lives inside the circle of all circles an *afterthought?* Is the existence of the incarnate Son of God an afterword, plan "B," which God thought up and put into action after the failure of plan "A" in Adam? Is Jesus Christ a mere footnote to the Fall of Adam, a footnote that would have never been needed or written if Adam had not taken his plunge into ruin? Or is Jesus the secret plan of the Holy Trinity from all eternity? Is Jesus Christ, seated at the Father's side, the eternal Word of God in and through and by and for whom all things were created? I tell you, the ascension of the incarnate Son was on the books in heaven before Adam, and Adam's fall, were even ideas in God's mind.

First, there is the Holy Trinity. Then there is the stunning decision of the Father, Son and Spirit to include us in the Trinitarian life through the ascension. As St. Paul says, the Father *predestined* us to adoption as sons and daughters *through* Jesus Christ (Ephesians 1:5). How can you predestine the human race to adoption *through* Jesus Christ if Jesus Christ is not even to become human unless Adam falls into sin? We have grossly underestimated the place of Jesus Christ in the whole scheme of things. Shame on us! He is the alpha and the omega, not a footnote. Jesus Christ does not fit into Adam's world.

Adam fits into Jesus Christ's world.

> Therefore, do not be ashamed of the testimony of our
> Lord, or of me His prisoner; but join with me in suf-
> fering for the gospel according to the power of God,
> who has saved us, not according to our works, but
> according to His own purpose and grace which was
> granted us *in Christ Jesus* from *all eternity*
> (2 Timothy 1:8-9).

First the Trinity and the beautiful and abounding fellowship of the
Father, Son and Spirit, then the stunning plan of our adoption through
the ascension of the incarnate Son of God. And only within this context comes the creation of the universe, which sets the stage upon
which the drama of the Triune God and of our adoption in Jesus
Christ will be played out. And within this context comes Adam, a
mere man, who is given a place in the history of Jesus Christ, a place
in preparation for the incarnation and the ascension of the incarnate
Son. The Son of God was already on the road to incarnation and to
ascension before the universe was called into being. Before creation,
our adoption–and its accomplishment in the ascension of the incarnate Son–was raised as the banner of all banners in highest heaven.

Most of the older Protestant theologies begin their discussions of
the death of Jesus not with the Trinity and the staggering plan of our
adoption, but with the holiness of God and the law, and with human
failure and the problem of sin. They superimpose a legal structure
over the heart of the Triune God and expound the death of Jesus under
the rubric of law and justice, guilt and punishment. But such an
approach eclipses the Trinity and the eternal purpose of the Triune
God for us, and thus utterly betrays the fact that there is something
much more ancient about God's relationship with human beings than
the law.

Before there was ever any law, there was the Trinity and the irrepressible life and fellowship and joy of the Triune God. Then there
was the decision to give human beings a place in the Trinitarian life
through Jesus Christ. The eternal purpose of the Triune God is not to
place us under law and turn us into religious legalists; it is to include
us in their relationship, and give us a place in their shared life and fel-

lowship and joy. If we must speak in terms of law, then we must say that the law of this universe is the primal decision of the Father, Son and Spirit to give humanity a place in the Trinitarian life through Jesus Christ.

The first thing to be said about the death of Jesus Christ, therefore, is that his death figures into the larger and stunning plan of the Triune God to include us in the Trinitarian life. He was predestined to be the mediator between God and humanity, the one in whom nothing less than the Trinitarian life of God would be united with human existence. Jesus' coming and his death are the living expression of the unwavering and single-minded devotion of the Father to His dreams for our adoption. The reality that drives the coming of Jesus Christ, and pushes him even to the cross, is the relentless and determined passion of the Father to have us as His beloved children. He will not abandon us. It has never crossed the Father's mind to forsake His plans for us. Jesus is the proof.

The first word is Trinity, the second is ascension, and the third word is *sin,* the profound spiritual disease that infiltrated the human race in Adam. Sin, in the Bible, refers not only to the original act of treachery on the part of Adam and Eve, but to the whole quagmire of human brokenness and darkness, alienation and estrangement that took root inside human existence through Adam's false believing. The Bible tells us that Adam and Eve were created as the apex of all God's works and stood before God as the objects of His personal affection and great delight. They were created to walk with God, to participate in God's work, and they were given a real place within God's unfolding drama. *But* they listened to and believed the lie of the serpent, and in believing the lie, they distrusted God, and in that act of distrust and wrongheaded belief, they opened the door for evil to enter into God's good creation and find a foothold.

Through the unbelief of Adam and Eve, *darkness* infiltrated the scene of human history. And with that darkness, loneliness and fear, isolation and loss, guilt and sadness and sorrow set up shop inside the human soul. And within no time at all, brokenness and estrangement and frustration, anger and bitterness and depression, envy and jealousy and strife, gossip and slander and murder began to overtake human existence. Anxiety became the poisonous roux which permeated the whole dish of human life and relationships, and indeed of all creation. Darkness snatched the soul of man and began dragging Adam and Eve down into utter misery, so much so, as St. Athanasius said, that human beings began lapsing back into non-being and extinction.

What was God's response? What was the reaction of the Triune God to such a disaster? The response of the Father, Son and Spirit to Adam's plunge into ruin can be put into one word: *No!* In that *No!* echoes the eternal *Yes!* of the Trinity to us. Creation flows out of the fellowship of the Triune God, and out of the decision, the determined decision, to share the Triune life with us. That will of God for our blessing in Christ, that determined *Yes!* to us, translates into an intolerable *No!* in the teeth of the Fall. God is *for us* and therefore opposed–utterly, eternally and passionately opposed–to our destruction.

That opposition, that fiery and passionate and determined *No!* to the disaster of the Fall, is the proper understanding of the wrath of God. Wrath is not the opposite of love. Wrath is the love of God in action, in opposing action. It is precisely because the Triune God has spoken an eternal *Yes!* to the human race, a *Yes!* to life and fullness and joy for us, that the Fall and its disaster is met with a stout and intolerable *No!* "This is not acceptable. I did not create *you* to perish in the darkness, not *you*." Therein the dream of the ascension and of *our* adoption in Christ becomes riddled with pain and tears and death.

There are those who want us to believe that on the day Adam fell, God the Father was filled with a bloodthirsty anger that demanded punishment before He would even consider forgiveness. And they want us to believe that when Jesus Christ hung on the cross, the Father's anger and wrath were poured out upon him, instead of us. But that is to assume that the Father was changed by Adam's sin, and that His heart is now divided toward His creatures. I say to you, God does not change. Adam's plunge was met by the same God, and the by same determination to bless, and by the same passionate love that birthed creation in the first place. The Fall of Adam was met by the eternal Word of God. The love of the Father, Son and Spirit is as tireless and unflinching as it is determined and unyielding.

How is the one plan of the Triune God for our adoption in Jesus Christ to be accomplished *now,* in the context of Adam's Fall and the sheer disaster it sent rippling through the ocean of humanity? Jesus Christ stepped into human history with the ascension in his sights, but the road to ascension and to *our* adoption is now paved with pain and suffering and death. For how do you get from the Fall of Adam to the right hand of God the Father almighty? The only way is through death. The Fall must be undone. Adam must be thoroughly converted to God. Human existence, broken and estranged and perverted, must be radically circumcised and systematically recreated, utterly and thoroughly transformed, and bent back into right relationship with the Father.

Why did Jesus Christ die? What happened in his death? Jesus Christ died because the Father would not forsake us, because the Father had a dream for us that He would not abandon, because the love of the Father for us is endless and unflinching. And Jesus died because the only way to get from the Fall of Adam to the right hand of the Father was through the crucifixion of Adamic existence.

Jesus Christ did not go to the cross to change *God;* he went to the cross to change *us.* He did not die to appease the Father's anger or to heal the Father's divided heart. Jesus Christ went to the cross to call a halt to the Fall and undo it, to convert fallen Adamic existence to his Father, to systematically eliminate our estrangement, so that he could accomplish his Father's dream for our adoption in his ascension.

The price tag on his mission was 33 years of fire and trial, 33 years of temptation, with loud crying and tears. In the *incarnation*, the fellowship and life of the Holy Trinity established a bridgehead inside human alienation. In the *life* of Jesus Christ, the fellowship of the Holy Trinity began beating its way through the whole course of human sin and estrangement and alienation. The faithful and beloved Son entered into Adam's fallen world, but he steadfastly refused to be *fallen* in it. For 33 years he fought, moment by moment, blow by blow, hammering fallen Adamic existence back into real relationship with His Father.

What we see in Gethsemane, when Jesus falls on his face, the gut wrench of it all, the pain and overwhelming weight, the struggle, the passion, the agony, all of this is a window into the whole life of Christ. His whole life was a cross, as Calvin said. From the moment of his birth, he began paying the price of our liberation. His whole life was a harrowing ordeal of struggle, of suffering, of trial and tribulation and pain, as he penetrated deeper and deeper into human estrangement.

On the *cross,* Jesus Christ made contact with the Garden of Eden, contact with Adam and Eve hiding in fear, contact with the original sin, with the original lie and its darkness. There the Son of the Father plunged himself into the deepest abyss of human alienation, into the quagmire of darkness and human brokenness and estrangement. He baptized himself in the waters of Adam's fall.

There on the cross, he penetrated the last stronghold of darkness. There he walked into the utter depths of our alienation. There the intolerable *No!,* shouted by God the Father at the Fall of Adam, found its true fulfillment in Jesus' *Yes!* "Father, into Your hands I commend my spirit," as he took his final step into Adam's disaster. Jesus died—and the Fall of Adam died with him.

Brothers and sisters, that was the darkest of all moments in the history of the cosmos. But, then again, how could it be? For the darkness that infiltrated the scene of human history and wreaked such havoc upon the human race, on this day and in this moment, met the light of Trinitarian life in Jesus Christ on the cross of Calvary. How could the darkness win? As surely as the flip of a light switch dispels the darkness in our homes, so surely the light and life of the Triune God conquered darkness, and death itself, in this moment, in the very person of our blessed Lord Jesus Christ, the incarnate Son of God.

It is not called dark Friday; it is called *good* Friday. Amen.

Anselm, *Cur Deus Homo*. Edinburgh: John Grant, 1909.

Athanasius, *On the Incarnation of the Word of God*. London: A. R. Mowbray & Comp., reprint, 1963.

Aulen, Gustaf, *Christus Victor*. London: SPCK, 1950.

Barth, Karl, *Church Dogmatics*. Edinburgh: T & T Clark.
"The Miracle of Christmas." In *Church Dogmatics* 1/2, pp. 172-202.
"The Covenant as the Presupposition of Reconciliation." In *Church Dogmatics* IV/1, pp. 22-54.
"The Way of the Son of God into the Far Country." In *Church Dogmatics* IV/1, pp. 157-211.
"The Judge Judged in our Place." In *Church Dogmatics* IV/1, pp. 211-283.
"The Homecoming of the Son of Man." In *Church Dogmatics* IV/2, pp. 36-116.

Calvin, John, *The Institutes of the Christian Religion, Book II,* edited by John T. McNeill and translated by Ford Lewis Battles. Philadelphia: The Westminster Press, 1960

Campbell, John McLeod, *The Nature of the Atonement*. Reprint with Introduction by James B. Torrance. Grand Rapids: Wm. B. Eerdmans Publishing Company, 1996.

Forsyth, P. T., *The Work of Christ*. London: Hodder and Stoughton, reprint 1946.

Kruger, C. Baxter, *Parable of the Dancing God*. Jackson, Mississippi: Perichoresis Press, 1995.

Kruger, C. Baxter, *God Is For Us*. Jackson, Mississippi: Perichoresis Press, 1995.

Kruger, C. Baxter, *Home*. Jackson, Mississippi: Perichoresis Press, 1996.

Kruger, C. Baxter, *The Secret*. Jackson, Mississippi: Perichoresis Press, 1997.

Lewis, C. S., "The Weight of Glory." In *The Weight of Glory and Other Essays*. Grand Rapids: Eerdmans Publishing Company, 1965, pp. 1-15.

Lewis, C. S., *The Great Divorce*. New York: Collier Books, Macmillan Publishing Company, 1946.

Torrance, J.B., "The Vicarious Humanity of Christ." In *The Incarnation: Ecumenical Studies in the Nicene-Constantinopolitan Creed*, edited by T. F. Torrance, pp. 127-147. Edinburgh: The Handsel Press, 1981.

Torrance, J.B., *The Orthodox Way*. London: Mowbray, 1979.

Torrance, T. F., *The Mediation of Christ*. Grand Rapids: Eerdmans Publishing Comp., 1983.

Torrance, T. F., *Preaching Christ Today*. Grand Rapids: Wm. B. Eerdmans Publishing Co, 1994.

Torrance, T. F., *The Trinitarian Faith: The Evangelical Theology of the Ancient Catholic Church*. Edinburgh: T & T Clark, 1988.

Torrance, T. F., "The Atoning Obedience of Christ." *Moravian Theological Seminary Bulletin* (1959) pp. 65-81.

Torrance, T. F., "The Resurrection and the Person of Christ" and "The Resurrection and the Atoning Work of Christ." In *Space, Time and Resurrection*. Edinburgh: The Handsel Press, 1976, pp. 46-84.

Weinandy, Thomas G., *In the Likeness of Sinful Flesh*. Edinburgh: T & T Clark, 1993.